## Workforce Wellbeing

Keep yourself well please and then look after the rest of em!

Best wishes,

Karen Warren.

# Studymates

Algebra and Graphs

Better English (2ⁿᵈEd)

Better French (3ʳᵈEd)

Better French 2

Better German

Better Spanish

British History 1870-1918

Business Communication

Business Coaching

Calculus

Chemistry: As Chemistry Explained

Chemistry: Chemistry Calculations Explained
(3ʳᵈEd)

Crime Writing

European History

Genetics

Ghost Writing

Growing Workplace Champions

Hitler and Nazi Germany
(3ʳᵈEd)

Lenin, Stalin and Communist Russia (2ⁿᵈEd)

Marketing Principles for Business

Numeracy for Health Professionals

Numeracy for Health Professionals:
-Scientific Application

Organic Chemistry

Perfect Grammar

Plant Physiology

Practical Drama (2ⁿᵈEd)

Professional Writing

Project Management

Shakespeare

Social Anthropology (2ⁿᵈEd)

Starting to Write

Starting Statistics

Statistics for Social Sciences

Study Skills

Studying Poetry
(2ⁿᵈEd)

The Academic Essay (3ʳᵈEd)

The English
Reformation

The Theatre Makers
(2ⁿᵈEd)

Trigonometry

Understanding Algebra (2ⁿᵈEd)

Understanding Literature and Film (2ⁿᵈEd)

Understanding Maths (5ᵗʰEd)

Warfare 1792-1918

Workforce Wellbeing

Writing Crime Fiction

Writing for Children

Writing How to Articles and Books

Writing and Imagery

Writing Science Fiction

Writing Soap

Writing TV Scripts

Your Master's Thesis (2ⁿᵈEd)

Your Ph. D. Thesis

*Many other titles in preparation*

# Workforce Wellbeing

## *How to Build Organisational Strength and Resilience*

**Karen Warren**

## Declaration
The information contained in this book is given in good faith for the purposes of education.  Neither the author nor the publisher or any/all of their agents can be held responsible for outcomes from the implementation of concepts herein enclosed and readers are advised, where needed, to take professional advice.

© **2019 Karen Warren**

**978-1-84285-535-5**

**Studymates Publishing**

**Abergele LL22 7DY**

**The rights of the author have been asserted.**

Book Cover and Typesetting by **SHED MEDIA**

**Printed in Europe**

# Table of Contents

**Dedication** – To all the people I've worked with, line managed and coached.  Thank you for sharing your experiences and working lives with me.  This book has been built on our experiences.

**Author thanks:**

Thanks to Sandra D.  Without you Sandra, there would be no book.

The author can be contacted via her website at kw-innerstrength.com and will be happy to answer your questions.

# Introduction

Employers, leaders and managers[1] have a duty of care to their staff to ensure they're physically and mentally well to carry out their roles.

- Is that duty of care[2] demonstrated in your team or organisation?

- Is your workforce well and effective in everything they do?

- Do all your staff have clear job descriptions[3] to ensure their work responsibilities are defined and agreed by both parties as the role they're expected to carry out?

- If you don't have job descriptions, clearly defined objectives and expectations of performance and behaviour, how can staff be held to account if they don't meet those expectations?

Whether you're an employer, an experienced/new line manager, or are learning about business and line management, this book will guide you to the consistent approaches required to effectively manage staff performance, behaviour and attendance. Short-termism can lead to a lack of investment in the workforce, which can lead to a loss of organisational strength and resilience.  A failure to take a more strategic view of your business can lead to staff dis-engaging and walking away from your team and organisation[4].

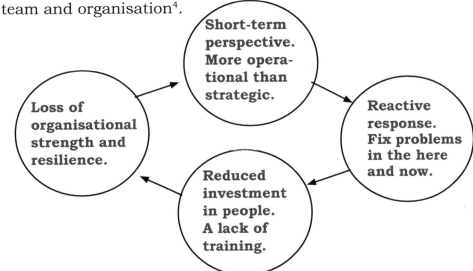

**Figure 1 – a short-term, operational approach to problem-solving**

© 2019 Karen Warren 9

Vacancies are then filled in a rush, so the best people aren't always recruited, and operational staff performance and behaviour issues can start to increase, particularly as experienced staff are relied upon more heavily to fill performance gaps.

If you're prepared to be open-minded and flexible about how your organisation works then change is quickly achievable. Figure 1 shows the potential impact of a short-term, operational approach. This cyclical effect can evolve very quickly as staff members recognise a lack of investment in their wellbeing and development.

If you're thinking "I haven't got time for this!" **then this book is for you**.

You will see why it's so important to know whether your workforce is well and you will have the tools to implement effective line management processes that will help build your organisational strength and resilience[5].

The key to that is culture change[6]; if your line managers are currently overloaded with their own work and receive no training[7], they'll struggle to exercise effective line management[8] and nothing will change.

Putting out an annual staff survey[9] is not making sure your workforce is well. You need to talk to people to fulfil your duty of care and to create an effective, engaged workforce[10] who smile as they come into work, most days and who will go the extra mile for you, their employer, leader or manager.

A staff survey can be a great way of monitoring progress but it's not a replacement for a range of forms of communication to include one-to-one meetings, team meetings, organisational events and performance reviews. It sounds overwhelming doesn't it? But it is achievable and that's almost exclusively by tapping into the talents of your existing workforce, who have the skills, knowledge and experience to make brilliant things happen if you, their employers, leaders and managers can create the right environment[11] to allow that to happen. This book will show you the steps needed so that you and your team can effect the changes needed and make those brilliant things happen.

So, let's get started!

*Karen Warren*

# Chapter 1

# Workforce Wellbeing – Why Does It Matter?

Your workforce is at the very core of your organisational strength and resilience[12]. Taking your responsibilities as an employer, leader or manager seriously and ensuring the consistent application of organisational policies[13] gives less room for complaint and dis-satisfaction from your staff. **The consistent application of organisational policies ensures a sense of equality in the treatment of staff.**

There is a concept called psychological safety[14]. This is a shared belief that the team is a safe place for interpersonal risk taking. In psychologically safe teams, members feel accepted and respected.

Psychological safety helps to:

- give a wider perspective on your workplace culture.

- support you to engage your staff.

- secure staff support in the development of your organisation.

**Organisational Strength and Resilience**
Is your workforce made up of people like this?

- People who are present because they need to pay their bills but aren't passionate about what they do.

- People who perform brilliantly but are never told that they do.

- People who don't perform well but are never told that they don't.

- People who call in sick quite often because they're not hugely in love with their job anyway.

- People who are stuck in their roles because you view them as a safe pair of hands and so you don't invest in their development.

- People who are using your organisation as a stepping-stone to other things.

***The organizational resilience tension quadrant[15] also gives an interesting insight into the complexities of business delivery and development.***

The people mentioned above, will not create a dynamic workforce who will strive to support your organisational strength and resilience!

If these employee types resonate with you, your organisation may be functional but it's most probably not effective, unless you and a small number of dedicated employees are plugging the gaps. It may be a long way off from being the best that it can be. You can change that positively.

Every organisation needs to know if their workforce is well. For example:

- To know if their employees are likely to respond favourably to a request to stay late at short notice or

- An ask for someone to step in to cover for a colleague.

If your workforce is well[16], the goodwill to do those things is likely to be there. If not, you may well be left doing the additional hours yourself. The days of 'I'm paying you so you should....' are gone and it says something  negative about your organisational culture if you do still adopt that approach. We live in more emotionally intelligent times, people won't always respond well when you need them if they haven't previously been treated well.

**Reciprocity**[17] is important and if you don't make an investment in your staff you cannot withdraw from the staff-employee 'bank account of goodwill'. If you don't treat them well, communicate positively with them and invest in their development they're less likely to be relied upon when times are demanding. If you don't invest, why should they?

**Employer Responsibility**
As an employer, you have a legal duty of care to your staff, which is should be defined in your organisational policies. These can include:

- **Recruitment and selection** including induction and probation arrangements.

- **Reward & benefits,** including pay structure, pension allowances and other benefits e.g. health insurance, gym membership.

- **Performance management**, including performance review processes, training, development and disciplinary procedures.

- **Absence management,** to include sickness, leave allowances and flexible working arrangements.

Policies should be readily available to your staff, via your website or an internal system to ensure they can clarify their rights and expectations. Policies work for you as an employer and the employee, when you both know what you can expect to happen in a specific situation.

The challenge is to make sure all your line managers are working consistently in line with your organisational policies and that they're making fair and equitable decisions based on those policies. A line manager's discretion is exactly that; decisions can be made with a holistic view of what is happening for a particular staff member but inconsistent decisions will give your workforce reason to complain. All people want is to be treated fairly but if a line manager appears to favour certain members of their team and is inconsistent in their decision-making, they may well lead to other team members dis-engaging, performing less effectively and becoming less reliable.

## Case Study

Stephen works in a team of eight staff and is line managed by his childhood friend, Phil. They went to school together, now play football in the same team and socialise together with their families. If Stephen asks Phil for time off the answer will invariably be "yeah, no problem mate!", which is different to the response other team members receive. They are asked the reason for their leave request and how their role will be covered in their absence. The same conversation doesn't take place between Phil and Stephen and this is known to the rest of the team. They find it frustrating. Stephen has taken time off in the past and made no effort to talk to his colleagues about what he's working on before he's been away and so there have been difficulties in trying to resolve customer queries in his absence.

Phil's finds it difficult to line manage Stephen, as they've known each other for years and spend time together outside of work. He knows that when Stephen asks for time off it's to support his Dad at medical appointments as his Mum is very ill. Stephen has asked that the rest of the team are not made aware of the situation as his Mum is very well known in the local community and very few people know about her illness.

## Task

*What should Phil and Stephen do? The apparent inconsistencies in the approach taken towards staff member's leave requests are creating frustrations in the team, which may well lead to a lack of engagement over time. What would you do if you were Phil?* As an employer or manager, your duty of care is to ensure your staff members can carry out their jobs. Historically, we used to think of health and wellbeing in terms of our physical capability but we now recognise the need to view people holistically, in terms of their physical, mental and emotional health.

## Challenges

While that's a more proactive and positive approach to ensuring the wellbeing of staff, it does create challenges. Should you, as an employer be responsible for helping someone who is struggling emotionally because they're having personal relationship problems? The source of the problem is not with you but the effect is seen in your organisation, so it's worth offering or sign-posting a staff member to support.

**Always remember, the problem is not yours,** you are supporting the staff member. You may pay for support services for that staff member, in order to help them get through a difficult time and to help them become more effective in their role again but what if it happens repeatedly? Whose problem is that?

Larger organisations can absorb the costs of support more readily but small and medium sized businesses will find that difficult. When do you reach the point of saying to your member of staff, 'I'm sorry but we need to take this down a capability route'? That will be a very difficult conversation but you're running a business, which is probably not a charity. It's very difficult to address these types of issues, especially when you really like and value the staff member, but it can and needs to happen.

The focus of this book is to ensure you know if your workforce is well; not to say you have to fix every employee who has a physical, mental or emotional difficulty. You need to work together to support a staff member but ultimately, they have to take personal responsibility for their wellbeing. If they're not physically, mentally or emotionally up to performing in their role then you both, as employer and the employee need to discuss how that situation can move forward.

If you're seen to support someone who clearly cannot perform in their role because, for instance they have been a loyal member of staff for many years, you run the risk of dis-engaging other staff. Could you make the same allowances for them? You can't afford to do it for everybody, your business would fail. By changing the individual's duties and paying them for that, you will show your care and consideration for someone in difficult times and demonstrate that you cannot pay people for work they're not able to do.

The way to negotiate your way through difficult situations is to talk to people, respectfully and appropriately, keeping privacy and confidentiality in mind at all times.

Talk to the individual and as appropriate, talk to their colleagues and other team members. Explain what the situation is, giving an appropriate level of detail, as agreed with the individual. Explain what's going to happen and the decisions that you've made.

If people don't like your decisions, they can talk to you separately and while you will listen to their concerns, your discretion as the line manager is final.

This is where the consistent application of your organisational policies is so vital. If you can support your decisions with the appropriate policy and show why discretion is required, you can stand up to a formal complaint should it be made. It sounds severe, but it's amazing what manner of complaints people will make. Backing up your decision-making with a sound knowledge of organisational policies and the support of senior colleagues if required, will reinforce your role which is important for your own wellbeing.

## Psychological Safety

Psychological safety is 'a shared belief that the team is safe for interpersonal risk taking'[18].

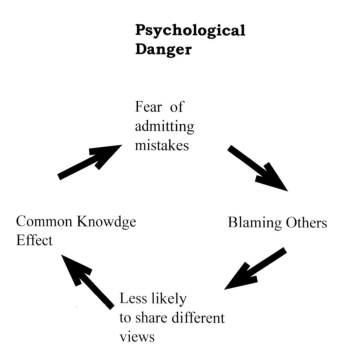

**Psychological Danger**

Fear of admitting mistakes

Blaming Others

Less likely to share different views

Common Knowdge Effect

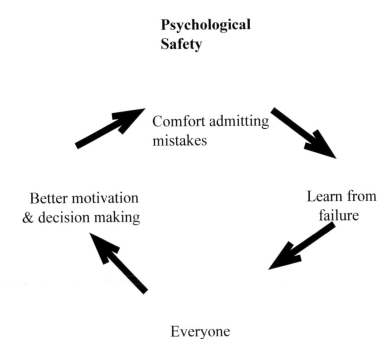

**Psychological
Safety**

Comfort admitting
mistakes

Learn from
failure

Better motivation
& decision making

Everyone
openly share sideas

## Figure 2 – Psychological Danger Vs Psychological Safety[19]

Figure 2 shows the differences between psychologically dangerous and psychologically safe workplace environments.
The 'common knowledge effect' defined as part of psychological
danger relates to how it can become known very quickly in
a team or organisation, that people do not admit their mistakes
or work together to resolve them. Psychological safety creates
an environment in which colleagues will work together to identify solutions to problems. It generates a culture of innovative,
open-minded thinking and effective decision-making, which

> *'Psychological safety creates an
> environment in which colleagues
> will work together to identify
> solutions to problems.'*

supports staff to feel comfortable to be honest if they make a
mistake.

**Task**

How would you describe your current working environment?

*Is it psychologically safe?*

If your workplace culture allows people to ask questions, challenge why you do things the way you do and admit they've made mistakes, you're engaging them to offer ideas and solutions which can support your organisational development, strength and resilience.

    The answers are often on the shop floor so whilst you might be a great employer, leader or manager you may be too

## *'The answers are often on the shop floor...'*

far away from the delivery aspect of your product or service in order to know the minutiae of what works so much more effectively with a very small change.

It's right that you are unaware of the minutiae, you can't lead your organisation and teams effectively if you do know that level of detail. Your job is to have a strategic overview. Their job is to implement the day to day minutiae.

    That's why you employ these people, so by asking them what they think and having an open environment to discuss options, you can develop two-way communication between staff and leaders.  You recognise your teams as the experts at what they're doing and ask them to help you to develop the organisation together. There's true strength in that approach.  If you think your team are idiots, they'll probably behave like they are and you will definitely be missing out on their talents[20].

    If a staff member puts forward a suggestion, don't tell

## *'You recognise your teams as the experts at what they're doing and ask them to help you to develop the organisation together'.*

them the proverbial fifty reasons why it won't work, try to make your feedback more constructive.  Ultimately a suggestion might not work but if you show it's been given consideration and explain why it won't work, you can secure the continued engagement of the staff member. Remember, their next idea could be a diamond!

> *"If everyone is moving forward together, then success takes care of itself."* **– Henry Ford**

By creating a psychologically safe environment you will get the best out of your staff and then they might stay late when you receive a last-minute order at 4.30pm which needs to go out that day, or your organisational equivalent of that situation.

> *"Teamwork is the ability to work together toward a common vision. The ability to direct individual accomplishments toward organizational objectives. It is the fuel that allows common people to attain uncommon results."* **– Andrew Carnegie**

After reading this chapter, think about your own approach to leadership and management.

Do you:

- fulfil your duty of care towards your staff,

- treat them fairly and consistently, and

- promote a culture where honesty, being open and making suggestions for change allows your staff to thrive?

Embedding these approaches into your management style can boost your organisational strength and resilience very quickly and make your staff feel that you value their contributions.

When staff feel valued their engagement level increases significantly,
Think about the changes you need to make to build and embed
that culture into your team or organisation.

# Chapter 2 -
# Workforce Wellbeing – What Does It Look Like?

The performance and behaviour of engaged[21] and dis-engaged staff and the impact of their performance and behaviours on the rest of the workforce is key to the development of workforce wellbeing.

A lack of challenge to unacceptable behaviour and performance can lead to a decline into a negative workplace culture very quickly[22]. It's much harder to reverse that trend once it's developed. By tackling issues quickly, you can earn the respect of other staff members and demonstrate that unacceptable performance and behaviours will be dealt with effectively.

## Engaged Staff

Engaged staff come to work. Consistently, they will:

- Turn up on time.

- Work enthusiastically and professionally while they're in work.

- Proactively offer alternatives if they're unable to come into work, for example, due to sickness.

- Make suggestions for change to improve processes.

- Sustain your organisational strength and resilience.

- Keep you informed about how things are progressing regarding personal issues that may affect their work and will endeavour to stay well to fulfil their work commitments.

- Proactively engage in performance reviews and objective setting.

- Be reliable, engage well with other employees and bring a positive energy into their work environment.

© 2019 Karen Warren

- Want to be in your organisation because they enjoy what they do.

- Show energy and commitment which supports and motivates the people around them.

- Be great ambassadors for your organisation and great role models to their colleagues and new staff.

Building a workforce of engaged staff won't happen magically without any effort from you as an employer, leader or manager. People come to work for a variety of reasons;

- They need to pay their rent/mortgage and bills.

- They have the right skills and experience to meet the demands of the role within the organisational field.

- They have areas for development which the role will help them to fulfil.

- The organisation has a structure that will offer opportunities for progression.

- The role in the organisation looks good on their CV.

- They've heard great or less positive things about your organisation that will allow them to progress and thrive or be lazy and coast.

**Task**

Consider your workforce in line with categories detailed in figure 3.Who are your engaged staff and who's less engaged? Who's performing well and less well?
Be very respectful of people's privacy as you complete this task and be very mindful of how the results are reported.

| Engaged, high performing and we're desperate to keep them. | Engaged, performing, great knowledge and reliability, we're really happy to keep them | Less engaged, just about performing, am happy to keep them if they respond to performance development | Not engaged, under-performing and having a negative effect on others. Would prefer not to keep them. |
|---|---|---|---|
| 15% | 65% | 15% | 5% |

**Figure 3 – Categorisation of Staff –**
**Engagement and Performance**

It may be a challenge to put every member of staff into just four categories but it will give you a sense of who's working effectively in your organisation or team and conversely who is not performing well. Be careful what you write down, remember staff have legal rights regarding the use of personal data. In larger organisations it will be useful to ask your line managers to complete this task for their teams as they know their staff members well and will have a more accurate sense of which category each person will fit into.

There is a need for caution, you may have staff who've personally had a really difficult year and who on paper look as if their attendance is quite poor. However, their line manager will know the details of that absence more specifically and so might place them in an engaged, high performing category despite their recent difficulties.

The percentages on the diagram show an aspiration for the breakdown of your workforce, in terms of engaged and performing staff. If your workforce doesn't align to that aspiration, you might need to think about your recruitment processes, and your organisational culture and performance management processes which we'll look at in greater detail in later chapters. Once you've defined your workforce into each of the categories, are you treating all of those staff members in the same way? This is not to suggest that only your engaged and performing staff members should be developed, but the trap you can fall into is that you spend more time with the people who are less engaged and not performing.

If you spend more of your time with the people who are performing less well, your more engaged and higher performing staff may walk away from you because they're not seeing you invest in their performance and development. If that does happen, the balance of your organisation (defined by the percentages in figure 3) can move towards a majority of less engaged and lower performing staff, and that can significantly impact your organisational strength and resilience.

People should be treated equitably, fairly and with respect[23]. You should be having a conversation with the staff members in all four of the categories. With an engaged, high performing staff member, you will be talking about next steps

## *'People should be treated equitably,...'*

and how the person wants to progress.

Hopefully there will be opportunities for progression in your own organisation but if there aren't, it's still useful to have those conversations. You can gain a sense of how long that staff member will stay with you and factor in contingency planning for when they're looking to move on.

No one wants to lose a highly valued staff member but they will leave eventually, so it's better for that to happen as a win-win, than have them leave feeling under-valued. They won't promote your organisation to other people and may well tell them of their own negative experiences which will impact on your profile as an employer of choice. People talk. They talk more about negative experiences than they do positive ones to vent their feelings, but if you develop and support a member of staff to leave your organisation, they will tell people about that and your employer profile will be raised.

These are long term investments but they do matter. Ten staff leaving an organisation with positive experiences might tell another four or five people about their great experiences. Whereas ten people leaving an organisation with negative experiences will be likely to tell at least ten other people each over time and news spreads. Negative stories are far more gossipworthy than positive ones so those ten will tell others and all the while, your employer profile is decreasing locally or nationally[24].

For staff in the engaged and performing category your conversations might focus on their development within the organisation and that can include training, job shadowing and partner engagement. Learning about what other staff members do in an organisation, particularly in a department unrelated to their own can build a greater understanding of the wider organisation and what other people do. It can be easy to focus solely on your own sphere of influence when you're working but job shadowing and cross-training staff members[25] can help them to look up and out across the wider organisation. That can help to build staff relationships and build conversations between departments which might be useful for the development of your organisation.

Small changes and improvements to processes and procedures can be highly effective in making your organisation function more smoothly and sometimes those changes will only be identified by bringing individuals in different departments together; to talk about what they do and to learn each others' roles. Departments often work in isolation so if you facilitate conversations between them through job shadowing and cross-training you will create the conditions for improvements to be identified. That can feel very empowering for your staff and in turn ensures their continued engagement. Win-win.

Partnership engagement is similar to job shadowing but it allows your staff to spend time, usually a half day, or a day with someone in a partner organisation, which might be a customer or provider of yours. The time spent supports the individual staff member's development and also supports the development of effective work relationships with those organisations. You might find that suggestions for change and improvements come back from those meetings, which will be useful for both organisations.

In the first instance, focus these development opportunities towards your more engaged and well-performing category staff, as they're ambassadors for your organisation while they're with your partner organisations. Engaged and well-performing staff are more likely to represent you, your culture and your business ethos well.

Conversations with less engaged and lower performing staff might focus on barriers to performance. Are there things that are affecting the individual's ability to perform well in their role, particularly if that person was a more engaged and higher performing member of staff previously? Support is very important if there are difficulties but it's also important that people understand the requirement to perform. Look at whether some form of adjustment to the person's work pattern or responsibilities will support them through a difficult time. Most people will respond well to that support and appreciate the opportunity to make their life a bit easier for a while[26]. They may not be able to stay on their current level of pay though, for reduced hours for instance so that will need a conversation and possibly sign-posting to other forms of support to ensure the individual can negotiate their way through difficulties with a range of options for support.

Staff who are not engaged and are not performing can have a hugely detrimental impact on your organisation for a number of reasons[27]. Their attendance can fluctuate greatly and while other staff may prefer it if they're not in, they are still being paid to work so it's important that they're clear on what's wrong, in terms of:

• their performance or behaviour.

• what's expected of them.

• how quickly an improvement is expected.

These conversations are not easy but if you don't have them, the effect on your other staff can be significant. If you're not seen to tackle issues of poor performance or behaviour, you are, in effect rewarding bad behaviour[28]. That can make other staff members question the validity of your organisational culture and values, and they may well, over time dis-engage.

Dealing with a lack of engagement and poor performance[29] takes time to do and time to take effect, so it can be hard for other staff members to see that issues are being addressed and that progress is being made, particularly if there are no apparent improvements. It's important to respect the privacy of the individual but it can be useful to explain to other colleagues that action is being taken. Progress might be slow, but it is being made, either for the staff member to improve or for them to be supported to leave the organisation. You might say "I recognise the problem and am taking appropriate action". If you receive a request for further details, confirm that you will not discuss the issue further, but that you're dealing with the issue appropriately. Respecting the staff member is key; that also sends a strong message to the rest of your workforce and balancing the amount of time you spend on the under-performing member of staff versus engaging with those who are performing well will show that you value them, even though you're dealing with a difficult situation.

Staff who are not engaged and performing poorly can erode the goodwill of their colleagues[30] so it's important you don't allow situations to continue over a long period. Dealing with a situation quickly, however difficult that conversation is, will ensure everyone is clear about what is acceptable and unacceptable in terms of performance and behaviour. If you're seen to deal with difficulties effectively you're much more likely to retain the respect of other staff. We all know that difficult situations arise, you can't always anticipate them but you can control your response to them and if other staff see you act, that will send a strong message to them. That you're effective, assertive and prepared to tackle difficult situations as they arise. By leaving a difficult situation to fester, you show that you shy away from difficult conversations and that will not win the respect of your team.

**Disengaged Staff**
Disengaged staff are less consistent in their performance, attendance and behaviour.

They typically:

•      Attend less consistently and have higher rates of absence.

•      Work less effectively than their colleagues and are easily distracted from the requirements of their role.

•      Appear unconcerned about how their absence or poor work performance impacts other team members.

•      Are reluctant to discuss their performance, attendance or behaviour when challenged.

- Are less engaged in the process of performance reviews and objective setting.

- Perform well but demonstrate attitudes and behaviours which are disruptive.

- Are less likely to make suggestions for change which will improve processes and support your organisational strength and resilience.

- Are less likely to report personal difficulties which will impact on their work performance and engage with offers of support.

- Are less of a team player, solely focusing on their own role and less likely to offer support to others.

- Make it clear that they only come to work because they have to, which can create a negative cycle of behaviour.

People who think you, as an employer or manager need them, more than they need you can become dis-engaged because they may feel:

- They're at the top of the development tree.

- They know more than their organisational leaders and so become bored with their work.

- Their work doesn't challenge them and so they may disrupt their workforce colleagues.

- There is a dependency on them, particularly if they're in a highly specialised role and so feel they can behave however they want to as you're unlikely to challenge them, because they think you won't be able to replace them.

Although the situation is challenging, it's not impossible to manage.   A quick, assertive and effective response is required to ensure the definitions of acceptable and unacceptable behaviour are clear.

Succession planning can be an effective way of managing those situations, either by asking the disruptive staff member to train others to ensure specific aspects of their role can be undertaken by other people or by asking them to look for apprenticeship opportunities, for instance to ensure a level of cover is available, in time. By focusing on succession planning you show that you're preparing for a time when the disruptive member of staff has departed. This scenario ensures they are aware they are replaceable and gives them an opportunity to reflect on their performance.

In order to sustain the organisation's strength and resilience it's necessary to gather as much of a disruptive staff member's knowledge, skills and experience as possible. The impact of their disruption will be reduced if knowledge and skills are transferred and you will retain a level of certainty that your organisation will continue to operate even if that person leaves very suddenly. If the staff member is being progressed through a disciplinary process, it's more likely that you'll see less productive work from them as the disciplinary action progresses but it's important for the engagement of other staff, that action is seen to be taken.

## The Cycle of Decline

If a staff member's poor performance or behaviour goes unchallenged, other staff may become lazy or dis-engaged as they see there are no apparent consequences for performing or behaving badly. Engaged and performing staff will be less than impressed by the negative change to your culture and may well look to leave. Lower performing staff will enjoy the drop in standards, feel more comfortable surrounded by people who think like they do and so they're less likely to leave. They're happy with a more negative culture that allows them to do an average job and spend time moaning about the organisation. That feels more comfortable for the lower performing staff.

Line managers may start to feel overwhelmed with the number of difficult conversations about performance and behaviour management they have to have[31], as well as trying to deal with their own work.
They have no time to work with and talk to the people who are

performing, they're just fire-fighting issues as they arise.

Talking to and developing the higher performing staff goes onto a well-intentioned to do list that never gets done and so the situation worsens as some of those people leave. Recruiting replacement staff then gets put to the top of the to do list and so now there isn't even time to talk to the staff who aren't performing as expected. Their behaviour just becomes the norm and continues. The cyclic of decline is under way.

Does this describe your organisation and workplace, or aspects of it? We have painted a very much worst-case scenario but it's easy to see how things can deteriorate very quickly and once a negative spiral of performance and behaviour starts it can be very difficult to stop the downward trend and reverse it. It is preferable if the downward spiral is never started but sometimes the change has happened over months and years and involved numerous changes to leadership teams. Defined expectations of what is and is not acceptable might have been inherited from organisations you've merged with and it can feel impossible to negotiate your way out of a legacy culture that has been embedded for many years. So, what do you do?

It will have taken time for an organisational culture to decline, with subtle changes happening in front of your eyes, which now collectively sit in front of you, which you regard in disbelief. You may ask, "How did it get to be like this?!" It will also take time to return your culture to a more positive state. However, you can affect change today. You can talk to your leadership colleagues to explain that this is the day that poor performance and behaviour being acceptable stops and use the categorisation of staff shown earlier to define how you're going to start the process of improvement and change.

Line managers; you can affect change with just your team, although that can be difficult if the culture across the rest of the organisation is very negative. But you can talk to them to:

- Explain that you want to facilitate change for them.

- Lead by example and ask them to be in the front line of that change.

As a team, you will:

---

- demonstrate role model behaviours[32],

- hold yourselves and others to account and,

- show how a more positive culture can be introduced.

You will need to work as a team because the transition will be challenging. Affecting change is not easy but if you and your team are up for the challenge, amazing things can happen and you can feel very proud of what you've achieved. Your work can then influence change across the rest of the organisation.

By managing people respectfully, assertively and effectively you will ensure that disengaged members of staff do not negatively impact the culture and wellbeing of your team. It can take a lot of energy to challenge people, monitor their performance and progress, and offer support but that's your role.

> *By managing people respectfully, .... you will ensure that disengaged ... staff do not negatively impact the culture and wellbeing of your team.*

You need to know that your workforce is well, performing effectively, behaving appropriately and supporting the strength and resilience of your organisation.

**Think about whether you're an engaged staff member. Which of the four categories would you put yourself in?**

Do you love what you do or are you there to pay the bills and nothing more? If you're not in the engaged and performing category you will struggle to inspire others to be there too. Think about your own level of motivation before considering how that will impact on your staff. Are you a highly effective and motivated team, who are recognised across your organisation as energetic, problem-solving and appreciative individuals? If not, a conversation in a team meeting about team perception might be useful, but you must lead that so think about where you're at first before you tackle anyone else's level of engagement.

# Chapter 3

# Developing a Culture of Wellbeing

It's important to set expectations for your organisational approach to wellbeing and demonstrate role model behaviours to gain the respect and engagement of your staff. Once you're in control of your own wellbeing you can define your expectations of others, to build a positive organisational culture[33] with appropriate challenge to those who are not demonstrating the behaviours you have defined. The answers are often within your workforce so consult and work with them to define your culture and the expectations of how staff members are treated. A culture which is imposed on a workforce is less likely to succeed. One which has involved its staff members in its development is much more likely to become embedded into everyday performance, language and behaviours.

Everyone can help to improve workplace culture and reduce the risk of psychological injury and 'because managers set the tone of the workplace, poor leadership is a significant contributor to psychological injury' [34].

You have the opportunity to establish the foundations of a great workforce wellbeing culture.

**Setting Expectations**
It's very easy to tell other people what to do but if role model behaviours aren't demonstrated, both the messages and the messenger can lose credibility. This will mean that good wellbeing behaviours will not be developed or embedded into your organisational culture.
The most common wellbeing offences are:

• Eating lunch at your desk.

• Answering calls and engaging in business conversations while you're eating your lunch at your desk.

• Not moving away from your desk regularly, for a comfort break, to make yourself a drink or check on your team if you sit away from them.

- Not stopping work at your desk from time-to-time to sit up and check your posture and break away from looking at the screen constantly.

- Sending and replying to emails in your own time.

Are you and your team guilty of these wellbeing offences? Have these practices become so normal in your work environment that they're never challenged? While the examples given are mainly based in an office environment and your work area may be different to that, they do translate to other workplaces. Take a break. Stop looking at a screen or doing the same repetitive work constantly. Even a one-minute break will allow your body to recover slightly from being stuck in one position or repeating the same movement for a period of time. Why do we not look after ourselves and value our wellbeing more?

We know the theory well; we talk about health, safety and wellbeing very readily but don't always put our words into action. We have legislation for health and safety but are not required to support the wellbeing of our workforce. As an employer, leader or manager you need to demonstrate your commitment to health, safety and wellbeing. Because if you don't, why should anyone else?

Setting expectations of how staff will behave in terms of their wellbeing[35] can start as soon as they join your organisation. Ideally it will be part of their induction[36]. You might say:

- We do expect you to take a proper break at lunchtime and move away from your desk or work area.

- We do promote the local facilities (whatever they may be) and suggest that you go outside for a walk, or another form of exercise during your break, weather permitting as that's good for your physical and mental wellbeing.

- There are a range of facilities available to you, for you to buy lunch or eat your own food away from your work area.

- There are a number of groups you can join, such as the walking group, running group and five-a-side football team, for instance.  We also have a rounders team in the summer.

- We do expect you to have regular breaks from your screen and to let us know if there are any adjustments required to your work area to make you more comfortable.

Those statements, alongside formal processes such as display screen equipment assessments[37] set a clear expectation that staff make wellbeing a priority in your organisation. Now you have to make sure staff see you follow that guidance. It's not one rule for you and another for everyone else.  You're not exempt from the advice and guidance you give to others because you're paid more than they are.  Quite the reverse in fact!  As an employer, leader or manager you have a responsibility to keep your staff well.  If you can't keep yourself well, how will your workforce make that a priority?

## *'... you have a responsibility to keep your staff well.'*

Setting expectations for wellbeing in your organisation needs to be an ongoing conversation as well as an induction conversation and might take the form of an agenda item in team and organisational meetings, for instance.  The question 'what are we doing to stay well?' can be useful to tease out ideas and suggestions of how team members are already staying well and how they can work together to make that happen.

The answers are often with the staff members already in your organisation; people who have an interest in sport for instance, nutrition, mindfulness and relaxation.  Ask people what their interests are and you will often find that wellbeing expertise already exists with your workforce, you don't always need to pay for external support.  Adding an element of competition can draw people in, particularly if workforce teams are competing against leadership teams!  The health and wellbeing initiatives detailed in appendix A offer ideas for what might work well in your organisation but it's also important that the conversation about wellbeing is an ongoing one, in one-to-one meetings, team meetings and at organisational events.

© 2019 Karen Warren

Creating a culture of wellbeing and consulting with staff does take time but if you take the time to do the leg work, potentially your workforce will be more engaged, healthy and well. Your absence rates will drop and productivity will increase. The time you invest in wellbeing will be returned to you, in time. Not this week or possibly next month but over a six to twelve-month period you can see very real returns on this work, which allows you to continue to build your organisational strength and resilience in the months and years to come. Culture change does take time but the cumulative effect of small changes, such as having conversations about wellbeing can have an instant effect on how the team or organisation is perceived by its staff members and that's valuable[38].

### Is It Running You or Are You Running It?

If you're in charge of an organisation, large multi-functional team or a smaller group of people, you're running it and them, aren't you? Or are you? Or are you responding to a huge variety of questions, demands, requests for support, complaints and suggestions for change from those people? And that's before you've started talking to any customers, potential customers, suppliers or potential suppliers! If you manage people, you're in the difficult position of trying to be many things to many people. Some of them will be happy with the responses they get from you but some may not be too happy and that will always be the case because you have your own work to do. You can't always spend as much time as staff members would like listening to their questions, demands, requests for support, complaints and suggestions for change. Making that clear is an important part of managing people's expectations of you, particularly time expectations. If you try to be all things to all people, that won't work. This is because you'll raise the expectation of the time you can give to workforce issues and so then your team will want more from you. People will always want more!

There has to be a balance, of you focusing on and completing your own work and making time available for your line management responsibilities. If you can stay in charge of that, by assertively and effectively managing peoples' requests for support then you will be running 'it'. What often happens though is that you end up fire-fighting everything; your own work and your line management responsibilities and at that point, 'it' is running you. If 'it' (your work) is running you, it's highly unlikely that you will have the time or inclination to focus on your own or your staff's wellbeing. So you and your team are likely to enter into more reactive styles of performance, behaviour and wellbeing.

The phrase 'is it running me, or am I running it?' can be useful. As you rush between meetings or return to your desk with your head whirling with all the things you need to do. As you feel overwhelmed and frustrated that you're not more in control of things. At that point, the phrase can be useful:

- **To make you stop.**

- **To make you sit down and take a breath.**

- **To make you think, about your own wellbeing.**

You can only control your response to events, you can't always control the events themselves. The workload will always keep coming and sometimes, the quicker you process the work, tasks, requests for change and responsibilities, the quicker more work will come in.
That's not a reason to deliberately deal with things slowly but once you have made a name for yourself by dealing with things efficiently and professionally, you will attract more work! Whilst some people thrive in busy and demanding environments you need to remember that you do need to rest. If you don't give yourself the time and space to rest, your physical, emotional and mental wellbeing can be affected.

### Limiting Beliefs
Have you considered if you have self- limiting beliefs[39] ? These are beliefs that constrain us in some way. Limiting beliefs can come from parents, family members, teachers and other people who have had a significant influence on us. For example, if as a younger person you were told your work was never good enough, you may still have that limiting belief embedded in your sub-conscious mind. This could then mean that you work to the detriment of your own physical and mental health because you believe the work you do is never good enough. If that's your belief, your self-esteem will be affected and it's high-

ly unlikely that you will prioritise your own wellbeing or your staff's.

If you feel that your work is never good enough, you'll probably think your staff's work isn't good enough either and that can quickly create a negative culture of performance, behaviour and wellbeing. If a team member is working hard but you, as their line manager, keep telling them that their performance isn't good enough, they'll probably stop trying pretty quickly. This protects their own wellbeing and so no one wins. Being driven, determined and hard-working are all great strengths but they can all become weaknesses if you over-do them and sometimes embedded limiting beliefs are the thing that makes you over-do them.

Having high standards is a great thing but please don't disable yourself and dis-engage the people you work with by constantly striving to meet unattainable goals, driven by embedded beliefs from years ago.

If the idea of limiting beliefs resonates with you, try to identify your beliefs. We all have those beliefs and identifying them can be the first step in taking control and minimizing their effect. This allows you to focus on more enabling and empowering beliefs about who you are today.

Remember you are not the person you once were so do not be disabled by things you were told years ago which probably weren't even true then, let alone now.

**Try this exercise:**

1. To identify your limiting beliefs, think about the people who haven't treated you well during your life. What did they say to you that might still be stuck in your mind, years later? Make a list of the people, what they said and the things that still resonate with you today. It may take time to make this list, especially if the messages are very difficult so give yourself some time to do it. Reflect on what you've noted and add to it over a period of days if more experiences come to mind.

   This can be a difficult exercise to complete as you may be re-connecting with negative emotions from the past so make sure your self care is good while you complete the exercise. Look after yourself well.

Once those negative experiences and limiting beliefs have been identified, move to the next step to re-frame the experiences and dis-connect from the negative emotions.

2.    Think about the following statements, in relation to each of the limiting beliefs you've identified.

•    Were their expectations of me realistic and kind?

•    Was what was said to me true?  If so, is it still true now or was it just because I was struggling at the time?

•    Was the person who made me feel bad being kind to me? Should they have been?

•    Could that person have had issues which made them be have in the way that they did?  (We're not looking to justify anyone's behaviour here but understanding why someone acted as they did can help diffuse the negative emotion from it).

•    What would you do and say if you could replay that event as an adult?

•    Can you reframe the event now and dis-connect from the negative emotion of it?

It can take a while for negative emotions to dissipate so keep running through the bullet points in order to re-frame the events and the limiting beliefs you were given.  Difficult events from the past will never be acceptable but by challenging the messages you were given, often in earlier life you can remove the limiting beliefs you carry today which can affect both your personal and professional lives.

Once you're happy to be in control of your own wellbeing you will be able to focus on the wellbeing of the people around you.  Not just in the workplace but with your family and friends too.  If this exercise has identified and re-connected you with negative emotions from the past and you're struggling to deal with them, it's worth accessing support in order to help you process and work through those difficulties.  You can access support via your G.P. (USA=M.D.), sometimes through work-place support arrangements or via independent coaches and therapists.

## Role Model Behaviours

You've built a positive wellbeing culture and people know what you expect from them in terms of managing and supporting their own wellbeing.  What happens now if you do see a staff member eating their lunch at their desk each day and taking calls?

## Case Study

Mark is a good worker and very much buys into workplace well-being.

He has supported the development of the wellbeing charter and lives an active life.  He often plays squash at lunchtime or goes for a walk to enjoy the fresh air and change of scenery.

Recently, you notice that Mark is working through his lunch-break, eating his lunch at his desk while he continues to work at his computer and answer calls if they come in.

## What action do you take to address Mark's behaviour?

Take a moment to think about this before you move on.  This is taking on the role of a reflective practitioner and this is a role that all professionals must master. It means thinking about the required outcomes and the strategies to achieve those out-comes.

An informal conversation, away from the immediate workspace tells you that Mark's working through his lunchbreak in order to leave early because his daughter is taking part in a theatre event for two weeks. He needs to drop her at a friend's house so they can travel to the theatre by train together.  While two weeks isn't a significant amount of time, you'd prefer that Mark does continue to have a break, to support his wellbeing.

As you don't have flexible work arrangements yet, you agree that he'll continue to take a break and work back the ad-ditional time, once his daughter's theatre event has finished. You re-iterate that if situations occur which impact on his working day, Mark can always talk to you about them, to try and find a solution that works for everyone.

Mark is happy that you noticed the change to his normal routine and took the time out to talk to him about it. By finding a solution that both parties are happy with, Mark continues to work well. He feels well because he has a break, plays squash or goes for a walk, and he respects and appreciates the support you have given him. By offering support, you have secured the continued commitment and engagement of a valued staff member by making a minor adjustment to working practices for a short period. Win-win[40].

Whatever you advocate, in terms of positive wellbeing behaviours you must personally demonstrate those behaviours. You're paid to work and may or may not be paid for your break but working through your lunch break, eating your lunch at your desk and answering calls while you're doing that, and sending and replying to emails during the evening and at weekends are not role model behaviours.

The implementation of policy is a responsibility of management and that means not simply paying lip service to that

## *'The implementation of policy is a responsibility management'*

policy. If you have a policy of positive wellbeing behaviours then members of staff need to see you enacting those polices on a day to day basis. Otherwise you are simply paying lip service to the policy. For example, if you tell people not to send emails outside of work time, but you continue to do that, you're sending very mixed messages about what you expect from people. If you send an email to a staff member on a Saturday, expecting them to reply on Monday when they're back in work, but they do reply that day, do you then continue to have an email conversation? Of course you do! Don't create situations by doing what you told your staff member not to do.

People can view sending and replying to emails outside of work time as a sign of their commitment, a badge of honour and sadly we've perpetuated that belief over the years.

But we're not in the second half of the twentieth century any more!

© 2019 Karen Warren

## *...we're not in the second half of the twentieth century any more!*

Working practices have changed so work effectively while you're at work and then spend valuable time doing other things while you're not there.  Rest and enjoy the time away from work.  That will keep you well and allow you to be so much more productive and effective while you're in work.  Having personally seen a senior manager send emails in the early hours of the morning over the weekend and another colleague work evenings and weekends because they were not productive while they were at work, it's clear that we have evolved some very dysfunctional behaviours which we appear to justify to ourselves.

Shine a light on your own work behaviours;

• Are you effective while you're at work?

• Are working additional hours?  If so, why?

Sometimes we're avoiding other life issues with work so think about what you would say to a loved one if they demonstrated the same work behaviours as you do.  Hold yourself to account on your own advice.   It's not easy is it!

It can be more difficult to define the boundaries of work if you work from home or have less formal working arrangements.  If you work 25 hours in a week for instance but can work those hours as and when it suits you, it can be difficult to ignore that nagging little voice in your head which is telling you to check your emails 'just to see what's going on' even when you've decided that you'll have a work-free morning to do something else.  Try to ignore that nagging little voice, otherwise you can get back into 'it's running me' territory very quickly and that's not good for your wellbeing or other people's.

Demonstrating role model behaviours and valuing your own wellbeing as well as that of your staff is great leadership.  Challenging less positive behaviours is good but it shouldn't be done in an open environment; "oh look everyone, Yvonne's eating her lunch at her desk, what a hero!", but as an informal conversation away from the immediate work area initially. Short term adjustments might be acceptable but keep checking back to ensure the correct behaviours are restored. As human beings we can get very settled into less positive behaviours and be very reluctant to change our ways when we're challenged on them. If people see themselves as an exception to the norm, that will go a long way to nudging them into better behaviours. If you're all doing it badly, no one will feel the need to make a change, however much theory you give them.

Kirsty used to eat her lunch at her desk but that was after she'd been for a walk for half an hour and people knew that's what she did. If someone apologised for interrupting her while she was eating her lunch, she could explain that she'd already had a break so it was OK to talk to people. You know what is and what isn't achievable for you and your organisation and by defining those expectations and talking about what role model behaviour looks like, you can affect positive change. If you expect other people to do it, you must role model that behaviour too. People will respect that, feel more inclined to mirror your actions and demonstrate their own role model behaviours. That creates a positive spiral of performance, behaviour

## *... you must role model that behaviour too. People will respect that...*

and wellbeing which adds to your organisational strength and resilience.

### Two-Way Communication

Ideas for health and wellbeing initiatives will often come from your workforce and not your leaders. That's great because it shows that people care enough about your organisation to offer suggestions based on their experiences of what works well. It's important that communication in your organisation is two-way[41], not just for wellbeing conversations but for all aspects of work. If people feel they're being dictated to by leaders who are not adhering to the ethos they're promoting, they are much less likely to do what's being asked of them and invest in proposed changes. And if the answers for health and wellbeing are mostly with your workforce, that's one thing they can take control of and move forward!  Give people the opportunity to promote their ideas, either with a suggestion box or via team meetings. A team meeting is a good way to float an idea with a smaller audience and gauge a response, before promoting it to the wider organisation.

If suggestions are received it's important to show that consideration has been given to each one, even if the final answer on it is a 'no'.  You can go back to the individual to explain why the suggestion cannot be progressed and tell the whole organisation about the suggestions you've had and why they are or are not feasible to implement.  That shows that you have respect for the suggestion made and the person who made it, and that may generate further discussions as to how that suggestion could work, possibly not for the whole organisation but for specific areas of it.

**Newsletters and Blogs**
Depending on the size of your organisation, two-way communication might be possible verbally but for larger organisations a weekly newsletter, blog or round up email will be useful, as long as you set the expectation that people need to read it, as that's an important way of ensuring communication between different areas of the organisation.  With that in mind, make it as short and to the point as possible!  You can also talk about it in your regular team meetings to check up on who is actually reading it.  Department heads can manage the completion of a 'meet the team' or 'what's on this month' article which gives details of what work's going on, what their successes are and what they need help with.

The crucial thing, if you use a newsletter, blog or email format to communicate with your teams, is that staff have a way of communicating back to you, with comments, questions

> *'The crucial thing... is*
> *that staff have a way of*
> *communicating back to you,'*

and suggestions for change.  This may be via one member of

staff who collates the feedback and directs it to the appropriate individual for a response but they need to make sure a response is given, which can sometimes be a frustrating thing to have to do when you're overwhelmed with work!  The point is that if you enable two-way communication across your organisation you will hear from people and that is useful.

**Feedback**
If you show that you consider people's feedback you will gain their respect and that will increase their level of engagement because they will feel that you value them[42].  Because you've shown that you do.  Of course it's easier not to bother because you're busy but you must decide whether you're going to build a more negative or positive culture of performance, behaviour and wellbeing.  Two-way communication is a key part of a more positive culture.

After reading this chapter, think about how well defined the expectations of wellbeing behaviours are in your team and organisation.
Are you, as a line manager:

- guilty of wellbeing offences which would make any conversation about wellbeing with your team a difficult one?

- Do you tell your team to behave in a certain way and then personally do the complete opposite?

- Are you demonstrating role model behaviours or are limiting beliefs affecting your own wellbeing and behaviours?

 It's a lot to think about but by analysing your own wellbeing behaviours you can support other people's development.  A conversation with the team is a great place to start and if you're guilty of those wellbeing offences, talking about why you are and the pressures of work can be a great way to help staff members open up about their own difficulties.

It can feel a bit like a therapy session to start with but a half hour discussion, followed by half an hour of developing a commitment to wellbeing for all staff for the next few weeks can be a great way to initiate change.  If we aim to achieve great wellbeing behaviours every day and achieve them most days, that's a great start.

# Chapter 4

# Maintaining a Culture of Wellbeing

Leadership is not just about the person in charge of the organisation or team. Leadership behaviours can be seen across your organisation and by re-framing your view of your workforce and engaging with people who have an interest and passion for health, wellbeing and self-development you can build momentum towards a stronger and more resilient organisation more quickly. The doubters will drain your energy but with great self care, for yourself and the willing few, the battle can be won!

## Leadership

What is leadership?[43] Definitions allude to being at the head of an organisation or team but leadership is also about behaviours which can be demonstrated by staff members throughout your organisation, whether those people have a defined leadership role or not. We tend to promote staff when they display leadership qualities, either in an operational or strategic sense but some people don't want to progress in that way, they just want to stay where they are and continue to do a good job. Does that mean they don't have those leadership qualities anymore, just because they don't want to be promoted? No, it doesn't mean that but it does mean that you can continue to utilise, (not exploit please), those skills to the benefit of that person's colleagues, team and the wider organisation. Leadership is not for everyone; some people don't want the responsibility and accountability of leadership but that doesn't mean that you won't see leadership qualities throughout your organisation at a range of levels.

## Task

Think about the leadership qualities and behaviours that are important to your team and your organisation. Now think about your team and wider workforce; are there staff members who demonstrate those behaviours but who don't want to be in leadership roles?

## Are You Utilising Their Skills Effectively?

When you spend some time defining leadership qualities and behaviours[44] and applying them across your workforce you can find that there are a lot more leadership qualities in your organisation than you first realised. Do not feel threatened. By having conversations with your staff, you will know the people who are ambitious and looking to progress, and those who are happy to continue in their roles and do a good job. For those people who are happy as they are, you can discuss how they can continue to develop in their roles, by undertaking job shadowing in other teams for instance and recognise their leadership behaviours, which will help to maintain their engagement. You can also think about how some of those leadership behaviours can be passed onto other staff, again possibly via job shadowing or mentoring opportunities.

Good leadership can be hard to define. Sometimes it's just something that feels right when you're in a great organisation. Two-way communication is key to that, as is recognising and not being threatened by the skills, experience and role model behaviours of others. You have employed these people, so it's a good reflection on you if they're amazing. If people don't want to be in leadership roles it doesn't mean they have no leadership qualities or behaviours to contribute to your organisation. Re-framing that in your mind can change the way you view your organisation and add to its strength and resilience.

## Staff Engagement

If you communicate with your workforce and find the staff who have a passion for workforce wellbeing, they can do much of the leg work to build and maintain that culture, with your support. A positive culture will only be sustained by role model behaviours from senior staff though, so while you can get rid of some

> *'A positive culture will only be sustained by role model behaviours from senior staff'*

of the leg work, you will need to actively demonstrate your support for the work that's being done. That doesn't have to mean that you train for the London Marathon, just that you acknowledge and show your appreciation for the work that's being done by others, with respect. If you talk about wellbeing with a sense of fun, that's how other people will view it. They can see if you don't really respect or value it. Sometimes a sense of fun is appropriate but it can undermine the level of effort that's being put in by people who are organising things if you get it wrong. If you dis-engage the organisers you can lose your leg work people so have a think about how you portray your view of wellbeing. Inwardly you can think what you like of course but outwardly your organisational strength and resilience will be maintained more effectively if you show how much you value the work that's being done by enthusiastic members of your workforce.

Staff engagement can take time to progress, particularly if you're moving from a more negative culture to a more positive one. The important thing is to keep going. There are six emotions that can be associated with change, which were developed into the Kubler-Ross Change Curve model[45].

The six emotions are:

- Shock.

- Denial.

- Anger

- Bargaining.

- Depression.

- Acceptance.

If a very negative culture has become embedded in your organisation, you may well see these emotions demonstrated as you make the transition to a more positive culture of wellbeing. Whatever your programmes, initiatives or events are, keep doing them. At first everyone may well think that it's someone's latest great idea and it might not generate much enthusiasm but with a consistent approach you will secure the more enthusiastic few initially and they can help you build a sustainable

© 2019 Karen Warren

change.  It can be hard though, people who are entrenched in less than positive behaviours will be very reluctant to change them.  They will be quite happy as they are and that's when you and your willing few need to dig deep and keep going.  Keep the emotions of the Kubler-Ross change curve model in mind, as they may help you rationalise some of the behaviours you see in response to change.

It can be frustrating to hear people referring to personal development such as building confidence and resilience, as 'softer skills' because the truth is, to change our ways, our habits and behaviours, to develop a more confident and resilient self takes a lot of hard work.  Organisational and workforce development are hard work too, it will take time[46].  Acknowledging that is important, to ensure you and the willing few support

## *'Organisational and workforce development ... will take time'*

each other to build the resilience to continue.  Your resilience will be tested but consistency, well-defined expectations and ongoing support are important.  You're sending a strong message to say that things will change, that you will be investing in the wellbeing of your workforce, mentally, physically and emotionally and while you might think that all staff members will be thrilled and delighted to hear that, some will not.

Those people might be in your less engaged and lower performing category from chapter 2 and their resistance may well make things difficult but if you and the willing few focus on those people in your more engaged and performing categories, you have greater chances of building success more quickly. Ultimately, we all have choices to make and if people don't like or appreciate your cultural changes they can move on to another organisation.  Their dis-satisfaction might be because you're looking to hold them to account for their performance and behaviours more effectively and assertively than you have in the past and so it may not be a terrible thing to lose them but bear in mind that we all have choices and part of people's resistance to change can show itself as threats to leave.

The important thing is to decide on the direction of where you want to go, secure in the reasons for why you're doing it and then stick with it.  If you wobble, and doubt yourself and the direction you're going in, your staff may well use that to sabotage progress. Sometimes, when people aren't happy in an organisation for whatever reason, it's easier to criticise everything that's going on there, than to proactively find the energy to look for another job and move. Those are the people who may well try to de-rail your progress. If you talk to them about their doubts and fears for change, you might be able to secure their commitment for what you're doing. The important thing is to 'call out' their behaviour quickly in order to minimise the level of disruption and delays to progress they can cause.

If the doubters, over time can see they're the exception to how most of your staff view your organisational changes, it will help to quieten their voices. There's nothing stronger than the momentum of positive change but it does take a while to build the momentum in the first place and that's when progress can feel like two steps forward and one, two or three steps back. Keep going! Keep giving out clear and consistent messages and actively supporting those people who are engaged with your plans, either because they want to be or have to be, to ensure the negative energy of the doubters doesn't win the day. You will get there but bear in mind that the doubters can be tenacious; they don't want change, it doesn't suit them to have to think about their wellbeing, performance and behaviour more proactively so you will need to pitch in, look after yourself and the willing few and access your most tenacious and resilient energy to get this done.

Focus on what your organisation or team will look like in six, twelve, eighteen months and two year's time and how you can be proud of what you've all achieved. As soon as you allow a pocket of negative behaviour to go unchallenged your progress has been dented. That might be just a small dent or a really big crater but people will be looking for your response to that negative behaviour and if they don't see one, they will doubt your commitment to the change. Positive culture change can take huge amounts of energy but the returns are worth it; to know your workforce is well, that you have strength and resilience across your teams and organisation is an amazing thing. But it will take time and effort to get there.

## Health and Wellbeing Initiatives
Health and wellbeing initiatives can bring people together, cre-

ate great kitchen conversations and help people get to know each other across the wider organisation. They can also improve morale, increase productivity and strengthen engagement[47]. Charities have identified two things that people will do quite happily in order to raise money; bake and exercise. Those two things can translate into health and wellbeing initiatives for your organisation beautifully.

Appendix A gives a range of suggestions for health and wellbeing initiatives which work well but it does pay to ask your workforce for their ideas as they will be more invested in making things happen once they're given the go ahead to proceed. The best health and wellbeing initiatives won't cost your organisation anything; the cost might be for a member of staff to buy some ingredients for a baking challenge for instance, which they will do in support of a charity. Staff members might need some time away from their desks to set things up for an event but the effort required is not usually significant. If you recognise peoples' efforts, they're more likely to repeat those efforts. If people feel exploited, used or overlooked they're very unlikely to put themselves out there again and are likely to dis-engage. At worst they can become critical of future efforts by other people.

The power of a simple 'thank you' is vast and should never be under-estimated. We don't always feel confident about saying 'thank you' and 'well done' but if it's sincere it doesn't really matter how you do it, as long as you do. Examples include:

- That's great (brilliant, really cool, amazing, fantastic, awesome), thanks

- You've done a great (cracking, brilliant, amazing) job there, thank you

- Well done, that looks fab (ace, great, brilliant)

- You're brilliant (great, fantastic, fab) at that, well done!

The important thing, when you give someone a compliment, is that it's about them not you. Saying "I couldn't have done it without you" is about you, whereas saying "thanks for all your hard work" is about them. It's a subtle difference but it's important in terms of engagement. It shows that you're recognising and valuing other peoples' efforts and not just thinking about yourself all the time, which is good leadership.

Is a health and wellbeing initiative only a success if every single person in the organisation takes part? No. You won't manage to get everyone involved in everything, you'll set yourself up for failure if you start with that intention. If 10% of your workforce show up to a range of lunchtime activities across a working week, is that success? Yes, it's a start and the important thing is to learn from what works and to keep trying. No one can criticise you for trying! And if people do criticise you, ask them what events they would like to see. That might give you ideas for next time.

We're all different and so what one person is hugely interested in will not raise an eyebrow from someone else, so variety is the key. If people say you're not catering to their interests, ask them what they want to do. If their request is not possible, if it requires a significant budget for instance, explain that to them and confirm that you'd be very interested to hear about an alternative to their suggestion, which is a no or low budget way of doing things. Leadership and facilitating change are not about having all the answers yourself, it's about engaging peo-

## 'Leadership and facilitating change are not about having all the answers yourself, it's about engaging people to find solutions.'

ple to find solutions. Those solutions will become embedded more quickly because they came from your workforce instead of an external source.

After reading this chapter, think about your leadership style and that of the other managers you work with. Does your collective leadership style encourage a sense of wellbeing and recognise the leadership qualities of other staff members across the organisation, even if those people are less ambitious? Are your ambitions towards a great culture of wellbeing a lone voice amongst less enthusiastic colleagues? Find the willing and enthusiastic few if you can, wherever they are in the workforce and find ways to build wellbeing into team and organisational language. Big change starts with small steps so by engaging a range of staff across the organisation, a new outlook towards wellbeing can be embedded fairly quickly to build momentum, enthusiasm and engagement from other staff members. That's the start of culture change.

# Chapter 5

# Identifying a Problem

Challenging poor performance[48] or behaviour is difficult but you can maximise your chances for success if you:

- prepare,

- identify specific evidence of the problem,

- find the right space and time to hold the conversation and

- listen well before agreeing a plan of action.

Very few of us want to have those difficult conversations but by planning, listening and allowing people to identify their own ways to improve you're more likely to ensure their future engagement.

What constitutes a problem in the workplace for you? Performance and behaviours can be very subjective and what is unacceptable for one person might not bother another. Consistency is the key; it's important that people see you demonstrate consistent behaviour and not treat your work 'pals' differently to other people in the team that you're not so friendly with. That approach can get you into difficulties when you need to have more serious conversations with a staff member about their behaviour. Your inconsistent approach, which you might adopt because you want to be friendly, may well undermine you further down the line. It's not to suggest that you manage your teams rigidly; line management discretion and flexibility are important as we all need a slightly different approach but working in line with your organisational policies and not showing favouritism earns you the respect required when situations need a very official response.

Think about your workplace values,[49] what's important to you?

For instance, punctuality might be really important to you but if you have a member of staff who has caring responsibilities for a relative and so needs some flexibility on what time they start work, a less rigid approach is appropriate. A conversation is usually enough to diffuse any anxieties on both sides so it's important to have those conversations with your teams. Get to know them and a little bit about their lives so you know what reasonable adjustments can be helpful. Your flexibility can secure your team's continued commitment and engagement. Win-win.

Is it acceptable to swear in your workplace? The use of strong language can be a very emotive subject and when we become stressed, angry or frustrated, we can use words that help us get rid of those emotional feelings. But is that acceptable for everyone? Or is there one rule for one work area and another rule for other work areas? Would you like your Reception team to use strong language with each other as a customer or some-one coming for an interview walks into your Reception area? Is it acceptable for people to use strong language that could be overheard if a colleague is on the phone? Ultimately, it's down to your personal values but it might be worth having a conver-sation with your team about acceptable and unacceptable be-haviours and making an agreement. Don't impose your rules without a discussion, that'll just frustrate people. Give them the opportunity to express their views. And if nine out of ten peo-ple in the team aren't worried about the use of strong language, just be more mindful about using it around the one person who does mind, be seen to respect their preference and talk about where strong language is unacceptable. Talk to your team about looking around them to check if someone is on the phone nearby and to think about whether they can be overheard.

A problem in the workplace[50] might be defined as:

- A performance problem, such as unacceptable standards of work, tasks not completed or deadlines not met.

- A behavioural problem, such as a poor attitude to colleagues, a disruptive presence in the work environment or a disrespectful approach to clients.

- An attendance problem, such as coming in late or leaving

early  with no explanation, increasing sickness absences or taking unauthorised leave.

If a member of staff excels in one area, in their performance for instance but their behaviours are unacceptable, you might be reluctant to tackle the behavioural problem, as that might impact on their performance.

However, if you don't tackle the problem, you will almost certainly store up trouble for a future time.  People who don't behave well are often waiting for someone to tackle them about it.  It can be a form of attention seeking so if you don't tackle their behaviour, those behaviours are likely to get worse over time as the staff member has not been challenged and so feel they have been given the green light to continue to behave badly.  While the individual might feel they're being given the OK to act badly, you're also sending a strong message to the staff members around that individual to confirm that you're not prepared to tackle their behaviour.  If you then try to tackle an issue with someone else, the example of another team member's poor behaviour will almost certainly be used against you and will weaken your argument for the behaviours you expect to see.

If you believe there is a problem with someone's performance, behaviour or attendance, talk to them to find out if there's a reason as to why the situation is presenting itself[51].  You might say, "are you OK?  You don't seem your usual chirpy self..." or something suitably supportive.  If you want to challenge the individual's performance you will need specific examples of when and how they have not met yours, or the organisation's expectations of their performance.  That's when your organisational policies can be so important, along with a defined culture and values if possible.  If you have clear definitions of what's expected, you can clearly state why the person's performance or behaviour are not acceptable.

You might say "I heard how you spoke to Rob (a colleague) the other day and I didn't feel that you were very respectful in how you did that.  We're committed to treating each other respectfully here, it's defined as part of our culture so can you talk to me about what was going on that day?".  It might be that Rob has been under-performing for a while and his colleagues are getting frustrated with correcting his mistakes and dealing with his unhappy customers, and so that was why the conversation went as it did. The conversation might then progress into the wider remit about how Rob's performance is being challenged and addressed, how role model behaviours are to be demonstrated by all staff, even in the most frustrating of times and how being able to stay calm is more effective. These situations can be hugely frustrating and in the moment, anyone can lose their temper and let their frustrations show but in one sense, that's when the other person is winning. Their poor performance or unacceptable behaviour has irritated a colleague sufficiently to make them lose their temper and show a lack of respect in front of other colleagues, potentially. That person and possibly others now need support to deal with Rob and to help them stay calm during difficult times.

If there are people in a workplace who do not perform as expected it might be that their behaviour has been 'normalised' to allow their line manager to avoid tackling the issue. We might hear statements such as "oh don't worry about Rob, he's always like that, just ignore him".

You may well know a few of those. The issue is that if a staff member is not performing, either in terms of their work or their behaviour there is an impact on their colleagues. If that issue is not seen to be addressed, your staff will have a view on how they think you should act and how they would deal with things if it were them. Ultimately that means your staff are losing respect for your leadership and may well start to dis-engage as a result. By not challenging poor performance or behaviour you're implying it's acceptable to under-perform or behave badly, so other staff might follow suit.

People like Rob, who are not performing in their role or are behaving badly can be intimidating to talk to, and so it can be challenging to address their performance issues. People usually know when they're behaving badly but if you call them out on it, they will often put a huge amount of energy into making life difficult for you, saying they're being treated unfairly and moving themselves into the role of a victim.

**Karpman's Drama Triangle**[52], shows how people can move between the roles of persecutor, victim and rescuer to create and sustain a drama, which very rarely allows issues to be resolved. People can exist happily in those roles for many years; there only becomes a problem when someone starts to feel unhappy in their role.  Change at that point requires reciprocal change in the other two roles and that's why people can find it so hard to remove themselves from situations, which very much suit the other people in the triangle, regardless of an overwhelming desire to change.

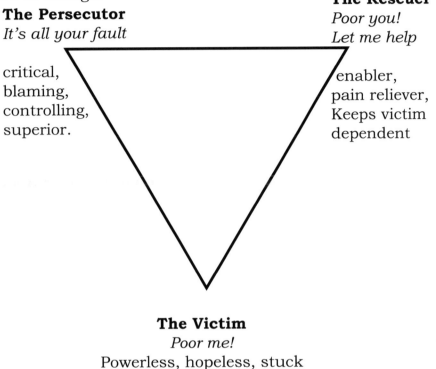

**The Persecutor**
*It's all your fault*

critical,
blaming,
controlling,
superior.

**The Rescuer**
*Poor you!*
*Let me help*

enabler,
pain reliever,
Keeps victim
dependent

**The Victim**
*Poor me!*
Powerless, hopeless, stuck

**Figure 4 – an illustration of Karpman's Drama Triangle**
You can find out more about The Karpman Drama Triangle and how it can affect you at https://www.karpmandramatriangle.com/

Using Rob as an example of someone who doesn't perform in the workplace, for whatever reason and is very defensive in his response when challenged on that, we can view him in the role of persecutor in the drama triangle.  If he then sees a consistently assertive response to his behaviour, which will require him to make changes to his behaviour he may well then move himself into the role of victim, spending time telling people about how badly he's being treated when he really hasn't done anything wrong, he feels.  Rescuers in your organisation may well listen to him and believe they're helping the situation when they listen to his complaints.  But actually, all it does is move the drama. Rob has now put you in the role of persecutor because he believes you're being mean to him; he is now the victim and colleagues believe they're adding value by taking on the rescuer role.

## Task

Does the drama triangle and the behaviour described resonate for the dynamics in your workforce? Think about how an awareness of the model can reframe your view and approach to challenging people's behaviour.

While it can be hugely difficult to unpick challenging situations, understanding the roles that people can take to create and sustain a drama is useful in planning your approach to address a situation. In Rob's situation the drama triangle could be used to explain the three roles and to ask if they in any way resonate with him. He might say 'no' but often people take in information at the time but it only resonates with them after a period of consideration, when it's settled in their mind, so Rob might think more about what you've discussed later on. If your staff are putting themselves in the role of the rescuer, it can be useful to have a conversation about the drama triangle to show how they're preventing change by sustaining the drama. Their intention is to be helpful of course but by using the drama triangle you can show them how their actions actually support the other two roles and don't allow people to progress, either to continue in your organisation or to leave it, if that's the best solution for all parties.

## Facilitating a Conversation

Any conversation which is intended to address, challenge, recognise, reward or celebrate an individual's performance should be undertaken away from their immediate work space. Further to a private conversation you may well talk more widely in front of other colleagues to recognise, reward and celebrate someone's performance but it's important to talk privately first. A more introverted staff member will not appreciate grand gestures, even if you like them as a more extroverted person and a more extroverted staff member might like a grand gesture even if that wouldn't be your preference as a more introverted person. Think about the individual's personality preference more than your own when recognising and rewarding their great work.  We'll talk about that in a later chapter.

Facilitating a conversation includes the following points:

- **Prepare** – define the problem, the evidence of it and what needs to happen.  During the conversation, the first thing you will do is listen so don't charge in with your prepared notes before you give the other person the chance to talk about how things are going.  They may well raise the issue you were looking to discuss anyway and that's a good way to start.  You can still use your evidence, define what the issue is and what needs to happen but it can be an easier conversation if you give the person the opportunity to highlight the problem first.

- **Give notice** that you want to have a conversation – it doesn't need to be days away, it's probably better if it's not, but a day or half a day's notice of a meeting can be useful, to give the person time to think about what you might want to talk to them about and to make their own preparations.  If you don't give people any time to prepare for a meeting, you may well not see the best of them in their responses.  If people feel like they're under attack, because they hear something that isn't expected, they're more likely to respond defensively.  Given time, even just a few hours of notice, that immediate defensive response is likely to have diffused somewhat and you're more likely to see a more constructive response to your feedback.

People will generally know whether they're performing well or not so they can anticipate the nature of your conversation and with notice, think about what they want to say.  Sometimes we do need to call out behaviours as they happen and so an immediate conversation is required but generally a period of notice is useful.  People's response to being asked for a meeting is to worry, even if they're performing well so do be mindful of that when you ask to speak to them.  There is a balance to be had, of giving someone time to think about how things have been and having time to prepare for the conversation, and worrying them unnecessarily for a week as you booked the meeting before you went on leave and gave them no idea as to what you want to talk about. It's not just about your diary, think about the impact on the other person too.

- Do you tell the staff member what you want to talk about? – this can be down to your personal preference and your knowledge of the individual but there can be a value in saying "I want to talk about how things are going". If things haven't been going well, the member of staff can start to think about that and plan their responses. Further aspects of giving notice of a meeting are considered in the next chapter.

- Arrange a suitable venue – whether you want to give positive or more challenging feedback, or offer support it's important that you find a space where the individual's privacy can be respected. Glass fronted offices and meeting rooms might look good aesthetically but they're not great if someone's feeling upset or angry. Think about how the conversation might progress and then pick an appropriate venue. Depending on your work-place, it can be difficult to access appropriate spaces to hold private conversations so think about what's avail-able off site locally as well. There are more and more office space rental companies out there so that might give you alternative options.

- Make sure there's enough time – while it's impossible to know how a conversation is going to progress, thinking that a potentially difficult conversation will take less than 20 minutes could be setting yourself up to fail. Sometimes it can take that long to get to the root of the problem and so to end the conversation there is highly unproductive. If an individual starts to open up as to why they've been struggling and you keep looking at your phone because you're expecting a call from an important client in the next 10 minutes, you will dis-engage them. Think about how you would like to be treated. This is a not a tick box exercise, you need to listen effectively and make a plan for how things can progress. Generally, that will take more than 20 minutes but if it doesn't, you'll get some time back, well done, and you can go and ask the rest of your staff how they're doing!

- Make sure you won't be interrupted – if you use some one's office  to have a conversation with a staff member, make sure they know not to come back until their room is available again or find another room.  It is their office but if you explain that you need to have a private conversation with a staff member, they will hopefully understand the need for no interruptions. If you suspect they might want to wander back in, find another room.  There's nothing more stressful than having a difficult conversation with someone while scanning the external environment for interruptions. You'll avoid a significant amount of stress for both parties if you find the right venue in the first place.

## Constructing Feedback[53]
Evidence is crucial, particularly if you're looking to challenge an individual's performance and/or behaviour.  The formula can be quite simple:

- You did (or didn't).....

- The impact of that was.....

- What I need to see is.....

The specifics of dates and times are important, as are the impact on you, other colleagues, customers, suppliers and the wider business.  If you say something like "you never get those reports out on time!" it won't mean anything to either of you so the member of staff will struggle to know what to do to improve, particularly if 80% of the time, they do get the reports out on time.  You need to be specific, particularly if there are only specific aspects of the person's work that you're not happy with. If they come away from your conversation thinking that you're not happy with any of their work because you've been too general in your feedback they may well start to dis-engage.  Further to your meeting, they might say "well I can't do anything

© 2019 Karen Warren    63

right apparently" and that can indicate the start of their disappointment about their lower performance levels, possibly directed at themselves inwardly but publicly articulated in a way that's directed at you. Other staff will wonder what's going on and that can disrupt their sense of wellbeing, as they think they might be next to receive some negative feedback.

The feedback 'sandwich' can sound a bit twee but wrapping a negative inside some more positive aspects of performance does have a value. Not to sugar coat your message but to make sure that the person comes away with a very clear impression of what they need to do to improve and which aspects of their work with which you're happy. Generally, people are not going to be pleased about being told that their performance or behaviour are not acceptable but they're unlikely to improve their work if you don't have that conversation with them. The longer you leave it, the harder it becomes to tackle the issue. People might not like the conversation but if you treat them with kindness and compassion, and respectfully explain what the problem is, most will accept your feedback. With specific information from you regarding what wasn't acceptable, why it wasn't acceptable and what the impact was, it's very hard not to accept the feedback.

**Effective Listening[54]**
There might be a reason why a member of staff is not performing as they normally would and that's why it's important to listen first before you dive in with a challenge around their performance or behaviour. If you have regular one-to-one meetings with staff members you'll probably know what's happening in term of work difficulties or wider issues in their personal life which might cause disruption to their performance or behaviour but if you're too busy to have those meetings, situations can evolve very quickly without you anticipating them. If a member of staff is experiencing poor health for instance, but is still well enough to be in work you might see changes to their tolerance levels. Behaviour that was seen just as office banter previously might be a trigger for them reacting badly to an innocent remark. It's important that you bear their situation in mind while also reiterating that as the behaviour was deemed to be acceptable before, it's their response that has changed. You can emphasise that you understand how their health difficul-

ties might be making them less tolerant but also suggest that they consider the impact of their behaviour on their colleagues. Reasonable adjustments, such as someone working from home one day a week, if that's feasible might help to alleviate some of the pressure an individual feels in the workplace when they're struggling with a health issue.

Effective listening can resolve a myriad of problems as people will often find their own solutions if you give them space and time to explore their options. The coaching and mentoring techniques, discussed in chapter nine, give a great structure for how you can listen effectively, direct the conversation with open questions and ask people what they would like to happen. Very few people are happy to perform poorly in their role.

If you're performing well, you're happier in your work and that's a win-win for everyone as you spend much of your life at work. Building a positive and effective culture where people know they can talk about their difficulties, will be held to account for not performing in line with expectations and will be celebrated for their achievements brings great organisational strength and resilience. Effective listening can underpin that culture; when people are heard, listened to and respected for their opinions, they engage and invest more positively in what they're doing. That can bring great rewards to your team and organisation.

## They Are Not You

Personal values are personal. If someone is explaining why they feel stressed and how that is impacting on their performance and behaviour, it doesn't matter whether you would be made anxious by that thing. This is about them, not you. Putting your personal values aside, you allow yourself to listen openly and without judgement. The Holmes and Rahe stress scale[55] defines the death of a spouse as the event that will cause a person the most significant amount of stress. If we adapt that to define the stressful event as the death of a loved one, and the loved one for an individual you work with is their pet, it doesn't matter whether you think their response to that death is appropriate or not. You still need to respond to the changes in their behaviour, give them time and space to explain how they're feeling and make suggestions for reasonable adjustments that might make their work more productive in the short and medium term.

Organisational policies will define your leave and special leave provisions, but you might also offer additional support at your own discretion. The consistent application of your organisational policies is important but using your discretion to offer support during a difficult time will also effectively ensure the continued engagement of your staff, as will regularly checking in on how people are as they work through difficult times.

It's important to be respectful to individuals. Be professional regarding who you speak to if you're expressing your dismay, about how someone is dealing with a difficult situation. Those conversations can leak out quite easily and may well get back to the individual concerned so your sincerity in subsequent conversations might well be questioned. At the very least you may well have secured the dis-engagement of that member of staff and that can affect team performance in a range of ways. It doesn't always matter what you think; it's the individual, their situation and your response to it that are important.

After reading this chapter, think about how you currently address performance, behaviour and attendance issues. Do you try to be nice about them or do you wade in with a critical voice that would intimidate the most resilient of people? Specific evidence of the issue is key, as is giving a staff member the space and time to explain the reason as to why a problem has occurred. In work and non-work environments, do you listen well or are you too busy and focused on your own actions? Think about how you would like to be treated, particularly if you were struggling and that was having an impact on your work performance. Sometimes people aren't struggling, they're just under-performing or behaving poorly but an effective conversation is key to understanding the reason why the issues have arisen. Once you both know that, you can move forward to define the improvements that need to be made.

# Chapter 6

# Difficult Conversations - Part One

Having difficult conversations[56] is not the way in which most people would prefer to spend their day at work but by tackling issues quickly and effectively, the need to have them will reduce over time as expectations will be clearly defined and staff members will know that issues will be tackled constructively. If an issue does occur, the staff member will be more likely to speak to you to identify the problem proactively or to confirm that they're struggling in some way, and will not wait for you to initiate a conversation as they might have previously. Their experience of your effective and compassionate approach gives them the confidence to adopt a more proactive approach. So while difficult conversations might seem like an all too regular occurrence as you start your transition to a culture of great wellbeing, the need to have them will reduce over time.

## Environment is Key

The right environment for a one-to-one conversation can be key to its success, whether the conversation is to deliver thanks and praise to someone for a great job or to challenge an aspect of their performance, behaviour or attendance. For a difficult conversation, it's essential that you think about the environment for the meeting and how it might progress. Not all situations can be anticipated but taking some time to consider the possible outcomes of the staff member's response might make things easier on both of you.

Is it possible or likely that the staff member will be upset and/or angry about what you're going to talk to them about? In that circumstance it's appropriate that you find a meeting room as far away from your immediate work space as possible to ensure the staff member has time to settle themselves before they have to go back into the work environment after the conversation. Most work environments are rife with gossip and someone leaving a meeting room, in the middle of their immediate work space, either in tears or looking very angry will set the rumour mill running very quickly. And that's not fair on the staff member.

© 2019 Karen Warren  **67**

Other staff might also overhear parts of the conversation if voices are raised and that's not good for anyone either.

Chapter 5 focused on the different aspects of facilitating a conversation:

- how to prepare for a one-to-one conversation.

- whether to give the staff member advance notice of the meeting.

- arranging a suitable venue.

- making sure there's enough time for an effective conversation to take place.

- ensuring there will be no interruptions during the course of the conversation.

In this chapter we focus on active listening and the importance of not  being distracted by other people in the workplace, while the difficult  conversation takes place.  These elements are very important to ensure you can be effective during a difficult conversation and that the privacy of the staff member is respected. However frustrated you feel about their drop in performance or behaviour it's important that your approach towards them is respectful.  There might be factors at play that you're not aware of and charging in with your frustrations will not lead to an effective conversation with positive outcomes.  It can be hard to keep your frustrations in check but if you lose your cool, you'll have to work even harder to recover a difficult situation.

Having said 'don't lose your cool' it can be useful for a staff member to understand the impact of their actions on you and the wider team but that needs to be said calmly to make it effective.  If you're repeatedly having to deal with a staff member for the same reason and are seeing no improvement it can be difficult to find the energy to be constructive in stating what you need from them.  There can be a value, after a period of time in indicating that you're running out of options and saying "I'm not sure how we can progress this".  You're looking for the staff member to make suggestions for change at that point and if they can't or won't engage in that process a more formal response might be appropriate.

Difficult conversations take time and add to your already heavy workload. Time for difficult conversations will never be factored into your workload so any need for them is an extra work pressure before you sit down with a staff member.

### *'Time for difficult conversations will never be factored into your workload...'*

Acknowledge your frustrations before you go into the meeting. A walk around the car park might be an effective way of giving you some time to vent your frustrations and plan your best approach. You're not made of wood and no one finds this work enjoyable but things will not improve unless you tackle situations effectively. Building the right environment for that conversation is key to its success. In chapter 5 giving advance notice of the meeting was considered, and that decision will very much be based on your judgement, your relationship with the staff member and your knowledge of them. If you know the staff member worries a lot it might be pertinent to give less notice to avoid raising their anxiety level but your judgement will be key to that decision. There is also a decision to be made as to whether you tell the staff member what you want to discuss and there are pros and cons for both approaches.

If you tell a staff member, two days before a meeting with them that you'd like to discuss their drop in performance for a specific reason, the quality of their reports for instance, you're likely to see one of two responses. Firstly, for the staff member to worry and take up time talking to other members of staff about whether your suspicions are true or secondly, to become very defensive and spend time gathering lots of evidence as to why your suspicions are not true. Both responses can waste time and so that can add to the argument for not giving advanced notice of what you'd like to discuss. Sometimes you might want a staff member to be mindful of the fact you want to speak to them, particularly if their performance or behaviour has been poor for some time. You might want someone to worry, to think more about their performance and behaviour for a couple of days before you speak to them but be mindful that they may waste time talking to other people and canvassing opinions for support. You should know your staff well, so your professional judgement will inform your decision.

As a new line manager, a suggested approach is, 'I'd like to speak to you on Thursday at 2pm about how things are going' and smile. Do not give an indication at that point that something is wrong. You don't know yet if there are reasons for the drop in performance or behaviour and so taking a friendly approach is professional and appropriate. A friendly approach will often result in a more productive conversation and putting your frustrations aside is key to that, as is demonstrating role model behaviours.

> *"The way a team plays as a whole determines its success. You may have the greatest bunch of individual stars in the world, but if they don't play together, the club won't be worth a dime."* – **Babe Ruth**

If you start the meeting with an informal conversation, it's important to make it clear early on that there is a specific reason for the meeting. You might say "so there is a specific reason why I wanted to talk to you today" and then move on to "how do you think things are going?". If the problem is more serious you might move directly into the specifics of what the problem are but it's important that you give the staff member an opportunity to respond, to give their side of the story and explain why they might be struggling. You might say "I've got some specific examples of when the reports didn't go out on time but can you talk to me about that first please? Are there things which have made that difficult?". If you're on their side and indicating that you appreciate that other factors might be involved in why deadlines have not been met, you show that you're open to discussing why the problem has occurred and can offer support to resolve it. It's impossible for you to know the intricacies of every work task for each of your team and so there may be problems that are easy to resolve, once you know about them. You might then have a conversation about why that issue hasn't been escalated to you before now and raise the staff member's awareness of what you expect from them. It doesn't have to be a hugely challenging conversation if you identify a problem, offer evidence to support your concerns and then keep an open mind to a solution. The challenge of maintaining a calm and friendly approach to these conversations is often more about your workload and the additional time pressure of needing to have the conversation. If you can put that aside temporarily, the outcome of the conversation can be achieved more readily.

> *"The dictionary is the only place that success comes before work."*
> **– Vince Lombardi Jr.**

Taking notes during a difficult conversation can be useful, particularly if things become heated. It can be useful to reflect on the content of discussions afterwards, once things have calmed down and if you don't take notes you might lose the finer details of the discussion. If the staff member has a defensive response to your claims it can take a while before they calm down enough to talk more constructively. The notes you take 20 or 30 minutes into the conversation are likely to be more useful than the defensive response you receive initially. Again, your judgement is key to this but be mindful that difficult conversations can become more formal disciplinary or capability proceedings in some instances and records of your conversations have a great value, to show your consistent approach and agreed goals.

As with more formal performance development or appraisal processes, reflecting back on performance and comments from previous meetings can be valuable for both parties and so taking notes is very much worth consideration. (Ensure you are mindful of the privacy of the individual.) Notes from one-to-one meetings, which include personal details should be kept secure and not left on your desk or in an open work space for other staff members to notice.

Effective listening, as defined in chapter 5 is key to managing a difficult conversation as is staying calm. If you feel yourself becoming frustrated or angry it might be worth taking time out and re-starting the meeting after a short break. There can be a value to saying "we're both getting frustrated now. Shall we stop, have a coffee and see if we can resolve things?". If you're both frustrated it's highly unlikely that you will find a satisfactory outcome to the conversation. By acknowledging both party's frustrations and suggesting a short break you're acknowledging that the situation is difficult for both of you. Sometimes staff will assume that you're fine in any situation, it suits them to think that, especially if they're feeling aggrieved, so by stating your frustration you can help them to widen their perspective on the situation and see the impact for both of you. Acknowledging your emotions can help to diffuse them so a short break might help you both to feel calmer and more positive about finding an effective solution to the problem.

At the end of any one-to-one meeting and a difficult conversation in particular, it's essential that you summarise the content of your discussions, to check understanding for both parties and confirm what needs to happen next. It might be useful to type up the summary and next steps, and email it to the staff member to give them something to refer back to. It shows that you're taking the situation seriously enough to make a formal record of the conversation and that can influence the staff member's behaviour more positively than leaving the meeting with no expectation of a written record of events and expectations for improvement. A follow up meeting must also be scheduled to check in on progress. That might be via a regular one-to-one meeting but it should be clear to both parties of when your next conversation will take place. During the follow up meeting you can check in on progress and consider improvements in line with your defined expectations.

> *"We think, mistakenly, that success is the result of the amount of time we put in at work, instead of the quality of time we put in."*
> **– Ariana Huffington**

## Assertive Communication – Verbal[57]

While the environment for a difficult conversation should be respectful to the staff member, in terms of finding a suitable location and delivering a professional and calm approach, your communication style should be assertive at all times. Assertive and aggressive communication are not the same thing but someone might perceive your assertive communication and behaviour as aggressive or very forceful if they have not been held to account for their performance or behaviour before. Your approach can still be assertive, in fact it needs to be but you might have to take things at a steady pace as a staff member adjusts to a different approach. Consistency is the key to helping someone adjust to a new management style. You can be friendly, helpful and assertive. There can be a perception that an assertive style is stern and serious and while sometimes that does need to be the case, in addressing more serious issues, a friendly and assertive style can be adopted at the start of your conversation.

If a staff member claims you're bullying them with your new approach try the following steps to help you stay in control of the situation.

• stay calm.

• reiterate the problem.

• confirm the evidence you have to back up your claims, what improvement you need to see and when it needs to be visible.

• Repeat these steps; continue to be kind, assertive and consistent.

With a changed approached to a lack of performance, a staff member's response can naturally be quite defensive. If you remain calm and deliver consistent messages, a staff member's reaction will usually settle and over time most staff members will respect the time you're taking to address an issue, with a kind, compassionate and assertive approach.

There are four communication styles[58];

• passive,

• passive aggressive,

• aggressive and

• assertive.

© 2019 Karen Warren

If you communicate in a way which is anything but assertive you're unlikely to achieve a satisfactory outcome for your difficult conversation.  Let's take a brief look at the characteristics of each communication style.

An individual with a passive communication style:

* will often fail to get results as they struggle to assert themselves.

* has a lack of maturity because real issues are never addressed.

* might say, "no one ever thinks about me"

An individual with a passive-aggressive communication style:

* will often mutter to themselves rather than confront the person or issue.

* will feel resentment while real issues are never addressed so they cannot mature.

* might say, "I'll make out that I'm going along with things but I'm not."

An individual with an aggressive communication style:

* will often try to dominate others.

* will blame others instead of owning their issues, and therefore are unable to mature.

* might say, "I'll get my way no matter what."

An individual with an assertive communication style:

* will state their needs and wants clearly, appropriately, and respectfully.

* are able to mature because they address issues and

problems as they arise.

- might say,"I can't control others but I can control myself."

Emotional maturity comes from assertive communication. Thinking about that might re-frame your conversations with staff.

## Task

Think about whether the four communication styles resonate with you, in terms of your own style and that of the people you work and share your life with. Focusing on a person's communication style can help you to understand their behaviour and consider why they might find improvements difficult.

Even if your communication style is assertive you might see the other styles from your staff members, which can create difficulties, particularly with a passive-aggressive style as individuals look to be co-operating when they're actually not. Ultimately, you can only control your own communication style and behaviours, so by demonstrating the effectiveness of assertive communication and behaviour you can give your team the opportunity to mirror your style. Not all of your team will follow your example but even the smallest of changes can make a difference to productivity and the working environment. Leading by example can take a lot of energy, especially if you don't see changes quickly but there is a value in sticking with it.

Using the communication styles as a team meeting topic can also raise people's awareness of the impact of their own communication style and can allow them to think about how they might be impacted by the styles of others.

It can take time to adjust to using a more assertive language but with practice you can make that change. Here are some tips:

- Make the language you use positive, constructive and helpful. You tend to get back what you give out.

- Don't fall into the 'but....' trap – "that was a great piece of work, thanks but don't lose momentum on it!" If it's a great piece of work, just say that and avoid saying 'but...'.

© 2019 Karen Warren

- Use 'will' and 'can', not 'would' and 'could'. 'Will' and 'can' indicate action whereas 'would' and 'could' only suggest a possibility of action which is less assertive.

- If the answer is 'no', say that! Or, "it's not no, it's just not now", for instance. It's important to manage people's expectations so you might say "I can't finish the report today but I will email it to you by tomorrow lunchtime". Saying 'no' is a method of blocking progress and is a negative response. Saying 'no' with a further proposal is an assertive and more proactive response.

The word 'supportive' can be defined as 'providing encouragement or emotional help' and the language you use with your staff can be assertive as well as supportive. There are often reasons why a staff member is under-performing or behaving in a way that you deem unacceptable and so a supportive approach in the first instance is appropriate. Your conversations may need to become more challenging if the staff member doesn't respond to your feedback and requirements for improvement but a supportive approach as you start your difficult conversation is the best approach. You will see very quickly if the staff member is responding to that or if a more challenging approach is required.

Remember, the answers rely on them. You have the details of the problem and the evidence to support that but the solution, in the first instance is with them. Your discussions and actions may become more collaborative as improvements are made but initially, you need to find out from the staff member what the underlying cause of the problem might be.

You might say:
- Why do you think this problem has developed?

- What's changed for you recently?

- Are there other factors effecting the outcome of your work? (That might bring in work or personal difficulties which will support your understanding as to why a problem exists).

- How well are you managing with your workload (for a performance problem) or with the rest of the team (for a behavioural problem)?

- What support would be useful to help you improve?

Empathy is important but sympathy is less helpful[59]. A sympathetic 'poor you' approach is less assertive and less likely to resolve an issue quickly. You might feel sorry for someone, particularly if they're struggling with health issues for instance or are supporting family or friends who are in difficult circumstances but a friendly and assertive response is still appropriate. Can that staff member take lots of paid time off, when other staff couldn't, just because you feel sorry for them? No.

It can be very difficult to manage situations when you feel sorry for the individual but you have to demonstrate an equitable approach to your other staff, in line with your organisational policies and with an element of line management discretion. It can be useful to ask yourself 'could I do this for everyone?'. If the answer to that is 'no' you might be being too generous in your support of a staff member. Difficult situations can usually be overcome by having ongoing conversations with the staff member and your organisational policies should allow provisions for unpaid leave, for instance if necessary. But ultimately, you cannot pay a staff member, long term if they're unable to work in their usual role and fulfil their working hours. Adjustments to hours and job responsibilities may be possible but it's important that other staff see a fair, equitable and supportive approach for a staff member in a difficult situation. They will monitor what concessions you make and will expect those to be available to them if they also find themselves in a difficult situation so consider that when you're feeling sorry for someone.

Listening more than you speak is a great approach to problem resolution as the answers are with the person with whom you're talking. The expression 'you have two ears and one mouth and should use them in that ratio' is a good thing to have in mind when you tackle a difficult conversation. Listening is a skill and listening without judgement can be very difficult but with practice you will see the benefits. Silence can also be an effective way of drawing out the emotional details of a problem.  If a staff member is upset and ranting, they're very unlikely to tell you their underlying fears readily.  Their reluctance will usually be that their worries and concerns will sound stupid if they say them out loud.  We can all think that, so try to create an environment where the staff member feels safe emotionally to talk about their worries and concerns.  Building trust can take time but with supportive language, open questions (as shown in appendix B), active listening and an open mind, you can create that environment.

You might say "tell me what you're worried about" but that will depend on the relationship you have with the staff member and the level of trust between you.  Calm communication is the most effective strategy.  Try to stay dis-connected emotionally, even if the staff member becomes emotional.  You're the parent in that scenario and they have become the child, temporarily.  If you both become emotional, you both move towards the child role and so nothing is going to get resolved.  If you have a close relationship with a staff member and do become upset during the course of your conversation, it's best to have a break, settle yourselves and then return to the conversation.

It can be important to know when you have reached the limit of your remit.  If a conversation is not progressing well or

## 'It can be important to know when you have reached the limit of your remit.'

needs additional input or support, you must say that.  If you struggle on, making statements and judgements beyond your remit you will reduce your credibility ultimately and may struggle to recover it with that staff member in the future.  Part of being assertive is knowing when to ask for help and being clear about that.  Taking the decision to halt the meeting to seek additional support or to bring a colleague into a subsequent meeting shows that you're clear about your remit and responsibilities, are taking the issue seriously and should earn respect from the staff member.  If they suggest, in a derogatory manner, that you're not able to deal with the issue on your own, you might say "no, I want to resolve this issue and we need some additional support, in order to do so".  That shows that you're both responsible for resolving the issue, not just you as the line manager.

Good verbal communication is key to managing a difficult conversation and sometimes that's not about what you say but the manner in which it is said. Talk in the first person, talk about the changes you, as an individual need to see, don't dilute your message by saying 'we'. Be respectful, show that you're listening and looking to find an underlying cause to the problem. Sticking a plaster on a problem will only resolve it short-term, particularly if your staff member is struggling with inputs or influence from other colleagues for instance, either in relation to their performance or behaviour. Pushing someone to agree that an issue is resolved when it's not will not result in a long-term solution.

Time pressures can often influence your approach; you feel that you don't have time for a more exploratory conversation, you just want to get the problem fixed! You can do that but your organisational strength and resilience will be improved if you make more of an investment in the staff member and the resolution of that problem. It'll take you more time to repeat the conversation and correct continued mistakes ultimately. Assertive statements, as part of a difficult conversation can include:

- "I will need to see an improvement (in your performance or behaviour)".

- "Your current (performance or behaviour) is unacceptable, it does need to improve".

- "It's not acceptable for you to treat your colleagues in this way".

- "It's not acceptable for you to make repeated mistakes".

- "There's an unacceptable impact (of your performance or behaviour) on the rest of the team and I'm not prepared for that to continue".

- "I require more from you".

- "It's unacceptable that you represent the organisation in

that way".

•    "There is a problem, however much you tell me there's not".

•    "I need you to talk to me about how you can make improvements".

•    "I expect to see changes very quickly".

**Assertive statements** are usually quite short and direct. They can still be said in a fairly friendly way but you're making your requirements clear. Sometimes you can falter and start to waffle at the end of an assertive statement as you feel self-conscious about the challenging element of what you've said. It can feel confrontational and that's not comfortable. It's more comfortable for things to be nice but if your organisational strength and resilience are being affected, it's important that you tackle issues directly and assertively.

Practice does help, so start small and work your way up to bigger statements if time allows. A great way to start is by practicing your use of "no, thanks" without any follow up explanation, which you might have felt compelled to provide in the past. You don't need to offer a further explanation, just the 'no, thanks' will do but it can feel uncomfortable at first. Practice will make it feel more comfortable.

## Assertive Communication – Body Language and Tone[60]

Good eye contact is key to assertive communication. If you need to deliver a difficult message to someone you need to look them straight in the eye and you can build the strength to do that by having the evidence of the problem with you. General statements like "you never do that properly!" will not land with the other person, it'll probably just dis-engage them from doing a good job in the future. By having specific examples of what the problem is and how it impacts the team for instance, you can look someone in the eye and explain what improvements are required.

An open posture and an open mind will help you to listen well and demonstrate your engagement in the process of understanding the issue, the reasons for it and making improvements. Chapter 9 focuses on active listening and how your posture and body language can show you're listening effectively. Your body language can give off subtle clues about how you feel generally, about how you feel specifically about the conversation you're having and whether you're desperately trying to leave the meeting and do something else. Try to be 'present' during a difficult conversation. It can be very challenging to do that, especially when the problem you're tackling is adding to an already overloaded work schedule, but by being present and listening well you're more likely to leave the meeting with an acceptable outcome and a plan for a follow up meeting. Thinking about the fifty other things you need to do that day, while you're having a difficult conversation will make you less effective.

Take a deep breath, try to put other work issues aside and focus on the problem and conversation you need to have. Your

## '*Take a deep breath, try to put other work issues aside and focus on the problem and conversation you need to have.*'

posture should be upright to demonstrate you're actively listening and your eyes need to stay on the person you're talking to generally. If you're looking at other things, either in the meeting room or outside it, you're showing that you're distracted and are not giving your full attention to the conversation. If you expect your staff member to pay attention, it's important that you do too. People vary in their body language styles and what might look like disinterest in one person might actually be their way of engaging but you know your staff best and can make that judgement. Leading by example is a great way to demonstrate what you expect and like to see but remember we do all have different preferences.

It's important that you use a calm and friendly tone of voice at the start of your conversation and it should remain that way throughout.

Assertive, calm and friendly is possible and preferable. Raising your voice indicates a loss of control and so you will be less effective at that point.  It's OK to say you're finding the situation frustrating but you still need to say that calmly.  When you feel anxious about a situation, such as having a difficult conversation with someone, you can sometimes talk too much to cover that nervousness.  Be mindful of that; less is definitely more in a difficult conversation.  You want the other person to think about why the problem exists and to offer solutions, and they can't always do that effectively if you're filling the conversation with supplementary chatter.

Nervousness can also cause the tone of your voice to rise and that can look like frustration to the other person.  Take a breath, settle yourself and say what you have to say calmly and effectively.  If tensions escalate between you there can be a value to saying "let's stop for a minute" and you might want to take a physical break at that point and leave the room.  "Shall we take a quick break and come back in a couple of minutes?".  That short break can give you both time to reduce your anxiety levels, try to see the other person's perspective and to reflect on your own behaviour.  Your brain is amazing; a lot can happen in two minutes in terms of your anxiety and emotional responses.  If it's useful to stop the conversation and take a break, then take the break.

## *'Your brain is amazing;...'*

If a staff member is experiencing difficulties and you feel sorry for them, be mindful that your tone is supportive and friendly, not patronising.  Anyone can experience difficulties and a supportive and friendly response during those times is valuable but in a work environment you're not their friend, you're their line manager.  You may actually be friends outside of work but make sure your response is appropriate to the context and environment of your conversation.  If you've gone out for a coffee socially and you're both upset, frustrated or angry about a situation, that's appropriate to that context but in a work environment your response must be professional and more emotionally detached.  Consider the question 'would I behave like this with all of my staff?'.  If the answer is 'no' it's worth stepping back and adjusting your behaviour and tone of voice.

If a staff member is becoming annoyed, frustrated or angry about a situation and their tone of voice is rising, you can explain that you share their frustrations, if that's appropriate but do not match their tone. By staying calm and acknowledging their frustrations, you give them the space to calm down more quickly. If both your voices are raised it's harder to de-escalate the situation and bring a calmer approach back to the conversation. You might say "I can see you're getting frustrated and I totally understand why that is but we're not going to resolve anything while you're feeling angry". It can be useful to let someone rant for a few minutes, that allows them to vent their frustrations and move forward but don't allow that to continue for too long. Your time is not being used effectively if you do allow that to happen and there will be less time available to find a solution to the issue. You might say "OK, so you've vented your feelings about what's happening but what are we going to do about it?".

It can be useful to ask yourself the question 'is this an effective use of our time?' when you're managing a difficult conversation. If there's a value to letting a staff member rant about a difficult situation for a few minutes, then allow them to vent their frustrations. But if they're still venting ten minutes later, you've lost control of the situation and need to put yourself back in control. A break may be useful at that point, or you might say "OK, we need to focus on a solution now".

In terms of your physical position, it's best that you're both sitting down during your difficult conversation, which sounds obvious. If, during the conversation one of you becomes frustrated and stands up do not continue the conversation until you're both seated again. In a position of authority, it can be tempting to stand up when speaking to someone but that sends a very strong message of hierarchy and 'I'm more important than you'. The best outcome from any difficult conversation is one that works for both of you. You can agree that

## *'The best outcome from any difficult conversation is one that works for both of you.'*

solution together. If you stand up whilst talking to a staff member who's seated, you send a message of 'the problem is yours and you need to find a solution'. In order to work collaboratively you will both need to be stood up or sat down and a seated position is usually more appropriate. Even in a heated discussion, your attention to the dynamics of both your physical positions can help to restore a calmer environment. You might say "You're frustrated. Sit down and take a moment before we carry on the conversation". Or you might say "I'm clearly frustrated, I've stood up! I'll sit down and calm down".

Standing over someone when you're speaking to them can be physically intimidating and perceived as an aggressive approach. People have different preferences in terms of their personal space but if you sit down beside them or invite them into a space where you can either both stand up or be sat down, you will be making the conversation more effective and a better use of both of your time. If you stand or sit next to someone and they move away from you, you're invading their personal space so move back slightly as well to show that you recognise that.

After reading this chapter, think about your communication style,
generally and particularly in terms of tackling a difficult conversation. Do you take an assertive approach to define the problem, the impact and the necessary improvements or do elements of the other communication styles resonate with you? Are workload pressures making your body language and ability to listen more closed which sends a clear message to the staff member that you'd rather be doing other things than addressing a problem with them? While of course that's probably true, an open and effective approach to a difficult conversation is one which will give you the most satisfactory outcome, so setting aside your
frustrations can help to resolve the issue more quickly, which will allow you to get back to the rest of your work more quickly.

# Chapter 7

## Influencing Change

Influencing a staff member's performance, behaviour or attendance can be difficult, particularly if the problem has existed for some time and has not been challenged. In that instance you might be portrayed as the villain as "there's never been a problem before!" and that can make a situation challenging, both while you're in a one-to-one conversation with the staff member and as you continue to work with them.

Sometimes, staff members who are struggling with a particular aspect of their role, behaviour or performance will welcome your support. They will appreciate the courage and energy it has taken for you to raise the issue with kindness and compassion, supported by specific evidence. Those people are much easier to help but what about the ones who are quite happy with their under-performance? How do we influence, persuade and nudge them into making changes? Staff who don't perceive there to be a problem when you clearly think there is one, are difficult to manage. A consistent and assertive approach is the key to them making changes.

Maslow's Hierarchy of Needs[61] (shown in appendix B) can help to explain people's resistance to change. Maslow defined employment as part of our need for safety and security but a salary supports a person's most basic physiological needs of food, water, shelter and clothing for instance. If you, as a line manager start to signal that there's a problem, two layers of need will be affected and there will be an impact on the staff member. Our sub-conscious minds are wired to detect threats and as a line manager indicating a problem to a staff member, you will be perceived as a threat.

### Scenario

Susan has been working for your organisation for 15 years, in a number of roles. She has been in her most recent role for five years and so is expected to know the role well, to know her customers and suppliers well and have good relationships with them. You expect that she knows the rest of the organisation well and has good relationships with staff in other departments. That seems a reasonable expectation.

You join the organisation as Susan's line manager and very quickly see that your expectations are not being met.  Susan does work quietly at her desk and looks to be busy but when you check in to see if a number of deadlines have been met, they have not.  You ask Susan why the deadlines have not been met and she says it doesn't really matter as the customers are used to her style and accept delivery, even when it's a bit late.  You ask about her relationship with her main customers and she says it's good, they send her a chocolate egg at Easter and a calendar at Christmas every year.  You arrange to meet Susan's main customers and find out that they're not at all happy, are increasingly frustrated by Susan's late delivery and are actively seeking alternative providers.  Across your own organisation, colleagues indicate that Susan's performance has always been a problem but her line managers have failed to tackle the issue.  Other staff are reluctant to engage with Susan as they often have to take phone calls from her angry customers, don't understand why she doesn't think there's a problem, and are frustrated that nothing appears to have been done to address the problem.

You arrange to meet Susan and explain that the situation needs to be improve.  You confirm the frustrations of her customers and colleagues, and explain her customers are looking to move to other providers as a result of her actions, but she insists things are OK.  You ask about previous performance reviews and she shows you her last two reviews which do not in any way indicate a problem.

At this point Susan remains calm and friendly in her responses to you.  You leave the meeting feeling slightly bewildered, having explained to Susan that you will need to look at this again and having arranged a meeting for the following week.  She seems quite happy with that decision.

At the moment, Susan does not believe there is a problem and that could be because she hasn't been made aware of the issue before and hasn't engaged with her customers sufficiently to know of their frustrations.  While you would hope that her own personal values would drive her to deliver on time, that does not seem to be the case and for some reason she is failing to acknowledge the issue.  There could be many reasons for Susan's poor performance, her refusal to acknowledge the issue and the impact of her actions on the wider organisational reputation and her colleagues.

In the next section we will focus on how the science of influence and persuasion can motivate Susan towards improved performance. One thing is certain with a staff member like Susan; change will not happen quickly and you might need to take formal steps to manage the situation to ensure your customers don't leave you. For this scenario we will assume that you manage to find a solution in the short-term that
satisfies your customers' requirements and that allows you to focus on improving Susan's performance.

## Influence and Persuasion

There are six short cuts to persuasion[62], some of which will be useful in managing the situation with a staff member like Susan.

- **Reciprocity** – people can feel an obligation to give when they receive.

If people are treated well, they will usually respect that and try to return that fair treatment to you, even if they're struggling. By taking a calm, friendly and assertive approach you can role model the behaviours you expect to see and while a staff member might not be thrilled that there's an issue with their performance or behaviour, they may feel an obligation to return that behaviour to you.

In our scenario, Susan is being paid to work to a defined standard and that includes meeting deadlines. There is a reciprocity between her salary and the standard of her work. Previously that standard has not been defined well enough by Susan's line managers but expectations and standards of work can be re-affirmed by you, her new line manager to indicate that her performance is unacceptable if she does not meet her deadlines and manage her customers' expectations effectively. By reinforcing the organisational impact of Susan's actions, in that her customers are looking for new suppliers, it can be demonstrated that her actions are unacceptable in terms of her personal performance and the wider organisation's reputational loss which is not why she is being paid.

In other aspects of reciprocity, you can focus on the impact of Susan's failure to meet deadlines on her colleagues, as they often take calls from her angry customers and find that frustrating. You might ask "how are your relationships with the rest of the team? Do you think you work well together?".

If Susan says 'yes', it's worth focusing on the impact on them of having to take calls from her dissatisfied customers. You might say "how would you feel if you had to take angry calls from another staff member's customer?".

A further aspect of reciprocity is that you're offering your time and support to improve a situation, which doesn't appear to have been done by previous line managers. They haven't challenged Susan on the problem, so at first you may well be viewed as the villain but over time, and with a consistent approach and messages from you, she may see the value of your investment in her improved performance, which will make her more likely to improve.

- **Scarcity**[63] – we want now what we may not be able to get in the future. While this principle of persuasion might not directly apply to Susan's situation, potentially you can demonstrate that her bonus will be reduced, for instance if her customers do move to other suppliers and the organisation's profits are affected.

- **Authority** – people will follow the lead of knowledgeable, credible experts.

While Susan is reluctant to acknowledge a problem and the impact on her customers, you have been employed as her line manager because you have the right skills and experience to fulfil that role. You have also been to meet her customers and can give anecdotal evidence of the impact of her actions on them. While she may be reluctant to accept your feedback, your credibility is the reason why the organisation employed you and so that cannot be questioned rationally. You may well also have experiences, possibly as a customer in a similar situation or as another supplier and can give other examples of similar situations and what the outcomes were, for the individual and the organisation.

You might need to say "I appreciate you don't think it's a problem, but it is. It's having an impact on our reputation, on your working relationship with your customers and the rest of the team". As Susan's line manager you have been given the authority to address this issue and if she doesn't respect that, more formal action may need to be taken. If Susan sees you demonstrate role model behaviours in the work environment generally and with her in one-to-one meetings specifically, she is more likely to respect your authority and make improvements. Sometimes people will say "I don't know how to improve!" and that might be a training issue or another aspect of their development which can be addressed by shadowing another member of staff for instance, preferably a high performing one. In that scenario, the important thing is to offer support, discuss the options for development and define the required improvements.

- **Consistency** – looking for and asking for commitments that can be made.

By giving a consistent message to Susan and requiring her to make defined improvements, with specific timescales you can influence her behaviour and persuade her to change. Sometimes people don't understand the impact of their under-performance or poor behaviours and so a joint visit to Susan's main customers in six month's time will encourage her to improve. At that point she will need to meet the people who have been impacted by her behaviour and it's likely that she will increase her efforts to meet their deadlines. You will need to attend those meetings with Susan and have conversations with the customers to frame the context of the visits, to identify improvements in the delivery process between your organisations, for instance. Please remember the purpose of the visit is not to shame Susan into making improvements, people must be allowed to keep their dignity. During the visit, you can ask a general question such as "what happens if we miss a deadline for delivery to you?".

You'll have given Susan time to improve her performance, over the last six months and so hopefully the response to that question will consolidate the need for her to deliver on time. Meeting customers and suppliers face to face and looking people in the eye can have a strong influence on behaviours, especially if the staff member doesn't think there's a problem or that they don't play an important part in the process of delivery.

With a consistent approach you can wear down the most

resilient of under-performers as giving the same message repeatedly, supported by clear evidence of what the problem is and the impact the situation is having on other people, makes it very hard for people not to change. If a staff member doesn't make improvements, following repeated attempts to identify the problem, its cause and impact, it will be necessary to adopt a more formal approach, of a disciplinary or capability route for instance. While it's always disappointing to get to this point with any staff member, you only have a certain amount of time available to manage performance issues and under-performing staff can take up much of that.

The risk is that you spend more of your time on managing under-performing staff and neglect your high performers who may then leave your team or organisation as a result. It can be very difficult to strike the right balance.

- **Liking** – people prefer to say yes to people they like.

If you have good relationships with your staff, they're more likely to follow your direction and work hard. However, you don't always need to have lots in common with your team for them to respect your authority. Staff members will like their line managers for different reasons. Some will want there to be a good connection and shared experiences, others will be happy that you give clear direction and leave them alone to get on with their jobs. If you earn your staff members' respect, they're more likely to like you and if they like and respect you, they're more likely to respond to a request for improvement. Tackling a staff member about a performance or behaviour issue is unlikely to increase how much they like you in the short-term, but the respect and liking they've had for you until now can influence their response to your feedback.

Sometimes, we all need time to think things through, so you might see a defensive response initially but a more considered response may follow later. You know your staff, so if they're behaving out of character and responding in a way that you don't expect, it's worth stopping a meeting and reconvening a day or two days later. You might say "I can see you're frustrated by what I've said, so let's leave it for now and we'll meet again tomorrow to talk about this further, after you've had time to think about it".

Giving clarification of the impact of a staff member's performance or behaviour on their colleagues can influence their inclination to improve if there are good relationships between team members and they like each other. We can all lose sight of our impact on others sometimes, particularly if we're feeling stressed or anxious, so making the impact clear to the staff member has a value. Very few people will not be affected by that news.

Building effective personal relationships with customers and suppliers can be a great way to give the impact of errors a more personal perspective. After a joint meeting with one of Susan's customers she might say "I really liked that lady, Rachel, she works in their Delivery team". She might say nothing else but we can assume that Susan is much more likely to make an increased effort to meet her customer's deadlines when she knows that Rachel, who she likes will be affected if she doesn't.

There are three factors of liking in terms of persuasion.
(Cialdini and Martin on You Tube [63B])

1.    We like people who are similar to us, so there's a value to sharing personal details and networking with people. For instance, you and a colleague might both love sport but if you don't talk on an informal basis it's unlikely that you'll discover that about each other.

2.    We like people who pay us compliments, so if someone does work hard and do a good job it's worth telling them that. "That's a great job, thanks" or "you're really good at that" will pay dividends over time as you're recognising hard work and great performance, and so often we've lost the habit of doing that.

3.    We like people who co-operate with us, so it's in Susan's interest to improve her performance to ensure you're more likely to co-operate with her when she makes a request that requires your discretion. You and Susan will like each other more if she co-operates with your requests for improvement and that may or may not be a motivator for her.

- **Consensus** – people will look to the actions and behaviours of others to determine their own.

If Susan knows that the other members of the team are performing well and consistently meeting their customer deadlines, she may feel a greater pressure to improve. You might say "no one else is consistently missing deadlines in the team. They're taking calls from your customers who aren't very happy but are working hard to manage their own customers' expectations more effectively". By understanding that the team would be happier, and possibly more likely to engage with Susan if she matched their performance level by keeping her customers happy by meeting their deadlines, Susan may be persuaded to make improvements. We'll return to Susan's performance issues later in chapter 9.

## Communication Styles - Directive Vs Non-Directive Communication

In chapter 6 we focused on four communication styles and we can also consider directive or non-directive styles of communication when trying to influence a staff member's performance or behaviour. At the most directive end of the spectrum, instructing a staff member on how to do something may be appropriate, particularly if they're new in their role but as staff increase in their experience and seniority a more supportive, non-directive approach can be more appropriate. Giving advice, offering guidance and making suggestions are directive approaches and can be a constructive way of directing a staff member. You're working together to find a solution, giving the staff member the space to think about their actions and the potential consequences but are also offering your knowledge, advice and experience to influence the outcome. A non-directive style is focused solely on the thoughts of the staff member, helping them to solve their own problems by facilitating their thinking, not doing it for them. By offering encouragement and support, asking questions to seek clarification and actively listening to the staff member describe their challenge, you provide a more non-directive style for them to consider a number of options, as identified by them. These are coaching approaches and so can seem less assertive than you will sometimes need to be but it's useful to think about how you communicate in a range of ways to inform your approach, to have lots of tools in your toolbox.

Both directive and non-directive approaches are suitable for influencing a change in a staff member's performance or behaviour and you will know them well enough to decide on the appropriate style. An awareness of the differences in the styles can be useful, particularly if you're feeling frustrated with a situation and think it would be much easier if you could just get on and deal with it yourself! You don't have time to do the work of your team members for them so by considering your approach to any conversation before you start it, with thoughts of 'am I going to direct this conversation or give them the time and space to find their own answers?', you will consciously make a decision on how you will facilitate the conversation.

A more directive style of communication will solve a staff member's problem for them. You might tell them what to do and they do it. In the short term that will fix the problem and sometimes you will need to take that approach. However, people don't always learn well if they can't see why something is a problem and how the consequences will affect others, so if time allows a more supportive and encouraging response can reap rewards. You might say, "how do you think that will affect your colleagues/customers/suppliers?". Giving feedback and providing a constructive challenge to suggestions from your staff member can be a great way to guide their thinking. Asking 'what if...' can be a great way of considering a plan of action to decide if it's a robust approach.

There are two aspects to delegation; the what and the how. If you dictate 'how' a piece of work is to be completed you reduce the scope for learning for your staff member. There might be particular constraints to be aware of, the structure of a report for instance but once the outputs of a piece of work are defined it's constructive to give the staff member the responsibility for how they deliver the work. That approach might make you uncomfortable, particularly if you've gotten used to dictating the 'what' and the 'how' but if you take a more hands-off approach you will see the benefits quite quickly.

Your staff are employed to undertake specific roles and hopefully they deliver against your defined expectations. By giving your staff the space to make their own decisions about how a piece of work is delivered you will see them grow and thrive. You will remain accountable for their work, as their line manager but they're responsible for their own remit and can be allowed to make decisions as to how they structure their day, for instance, or which work they focus on to meet specific deadlines. If a staff member is performing well in their role you should not need to dictate how a piece of work is completed. You might discuss it but what's important is that you accept that a staff member's approach might be different to yours and it doesn't mean that your approach is right, because you're the line manager and theirs is wrong. It's just a different approach.

It can be easy for us all to think "it would be better if you did it my way" but unless you intend to undertake all of the work of each of your staff members yourself, you will need to accept that they may deliver work in a style that's different to yours. As long as the output is as you agreed, you will need to find a way to tolerate those differences. As a line manager, particularly in times of pressure, it can be easy to adopt a more directive and dictatorial style. We've probably all done it and sometimes, it might just be what's required in a particular instance. But generally, you need to trust your staff to deliver the work you have agreed with them, to a defined standard. If you don't, you will dis-empower your staff, who may well dis-engage from you and their work responsibilities and then you may end up doing most of the work yourself anyway.

An effective line manager will direct their teams to achieve, not do their work for them. Micro-managing a staff member is not an effective approach; it shows that you don't trust their judgement, their skills and experience and feel the need to dictate the way in which their work should be completed. The term 'hero leadership'[64] defines a leader who believes they need to swoop in to save the day. Those leaders find their self-esteem from rescuing situations because other people, they feel, are not up to the job. If you think that way, you're not showing trust in your staff; in their skills and experience, and their ability to find solutions to challenges. That approach will not engage your staff or help you to build effective relationships with them. Why should they make the effort to find their own solutions when they know you will dictate the approach anyway? If you do not require your staff to find their own solutions, because you'll tell them what to do, you may well find them moving on from your team quite quickly. Hero leadership and micro-management lend themselves to parent-child style relationships with your staff and most of us, as adults won't appreciate that approach.

## Communicating with Influence

Directive influencing tends to be a one-way conversation with someone asserting a need, particularly when there is an urgency to a situation and you're the person with authority. You might say "I need you to....." or "change that immediately!". A collaborative approach is more of a two-way conversation; using your knowledge and experience, offering and seeking information to guide a staff member to a solution. You might say, "here's a suggestion, let's think if that will work" or "let's look at the solutions you've identified".

**Persuasive reasoning** is making a strong case for something, using evidence, policies or regulations to add to the weight of the argument. You might say, "the policy states that we need to...." or "the evidence suggests....". Persuasive reasoning can be useful in a team meeting setting, particularly if you're facilitating a conversation relating to change.

A charismatic or visionary style is where you inspire others to see a future vision that they will be part of. You might say, "imagine, in 18 months time, that we can...." or "I envisage the changes as...". This style can encourage creativity and big picture thinking. It's very useful when you want to influence staff members strategically and need to motivate others to share your thinking. Using this style at the start of a major change programme can secure the engagement of staff and encourage them to think beyond their day-to-day work activities.

**Communicating with influence** can secure an effective outcome quickly. Think about your style before you enter into a conversation with a staff member. Do you need to find an operational solution and is there time to think about what will work best? If so, a collaborative, non-directive style can work well in that instance. Do you need to find an operational solution within the hour? A directive approach is appropriate to resolve the issue but if possible, a follow up conversation to review what happened and think about how the issue can be dealt with differently in the future is useful.

If you direct people they're less likely to learn than if you facilitate their thinking, to find their own solutions. It does take time and sometimes that can be frustrating but your organisational strength and resilience will be sustained by effective staff members who think about how they deliver their work. If you do that thinking for them, the dependency on you increases and that reduces organisational strength and resilience. Staff respond well when you encourage them to find their own solutions, when you demonstrate your trust in their skills and abilities.

After reading this chapter, think about your communication style and whether it encourages your staff to find their own solutions or if you just tell them what to do. If you tell your team what to do you may well feel frustrated that they interrupt you all the time to ask you questions, but unless you step back and give them the time to find their own solutions, they will keep coming back to you for answers. What do they do when you're on leave, how do they find solutions then? As human beings we can be lazy; it can be easier to ask someone else than to find our own solutions so if you become that kind of line manager then you're perpetuating that cycle of behaviour and allowing your staff to drain your energy and not think for themselves. It takes longer to ask "what do you think you should do?" especially when you already know the answer yourself but staff will keep coming back to you for answers unless you encourage and support them to think more independently.

What influences you to make changes? Think about your own preferences and how you will influence the performance and behaviour of your staff members. Do you enjoy a directive communication style from others or do you prefer a less-directive, coaching style that helps you to find your own solutions? Consider whether your preferred styles are how you communicate with others and why there may be discrepancies between the two styles. Are stress and anxiety making you more directive to others, even though that's not your own preference? Talk to the team about the different methods of influence and communication to help tease out any problem areas and to strengthen your communication as a team.

# Chapter 8
# Difficult Conversations - Part Two

It's very easy to tell people what to do. To direct other people, tell them what they 'should' be doing and how they 'should' be behaving. To tell them what good wellbeing looks like and that they 'should' take a break at lunchtime but which they will never do. 'Should' is a stupid word; there are all sorts of things we all 'should' be doing but if we take responsibility for ourselves then we can talk about:

• the things we will do.

• the behaviours we will demonstrate.

• the wellbeing behaviours that we will adopt and look for others to adopt too.

An effective part of managing difficult conversations is to take responsibility for your own actions[65], be seen to sometimes succeed and sometimes fail at that and to talk about how it can be really challenging to balance a mix of conflicting priorities. If you talk about that to your teams, you're more likely to secure their engagement and a commitment to work hard. You have to be human with people in order for them to relate to you, so if you make out that you're perfect and never struggle, you may well find connecting with a staff member and working together to improve their performance and behaviour more difficult.

## Taking Responsibility – You and Them
You and your staff member both share a responsibility for the delivery of their role to meet a defined standard. In chapter 12 we focus on defining goals and objectives as part of a performance management process but the first requirement for any role is an up to date job description. If up to date job descriptions are not in place, staff members cannot be held to account if they don't meet expectations, in terms of carrying out their defined role, their performance or behaviour. As an employer or line manager you have a responsibility to your staff members to keep their job descriptions current, within reason. Updating a job description monthly is not the best use of anyone's time

and job descriptions will usually include a number of more generic responsibilities which allow an element of flexibility in the job role to be completed. Keeping job descriptions up to date should not disable you, as a manager or an employer but if job descriptions are years out of date, they will be of very little use to you when you try to hold a staff member to account for their performance or behaviour. An out of date job description may well be used as a form of defence against you if a performance or behavioural challenge is made, so you need to ensure 'your house is in order' before you start those difficult conversations.

As an employer or line manager, you have a responsibility to be consistent in your approach. In times of high pressure and stress it can be easy to respond with frustration when a staff member is not performing as you would expect them to, but demonstrating less positive behaviours, when you're planning to challenge a staff member on theirs will not win you any credibility. Deciding that something's a problem today, because you're feeling frustrated today, when you've let the same thing go unchallenged previously is not going to give out a consistent message.

If a staff member feels confused as to what is and what is not acceptable, they're likely to disengage and so their work performance might drop. As people, we like to know where we stand; to know what's deemed to be acceptable and unacceptable behaviour, and what's expected of us. Then, generally we'll work within those constraints. Problems can arise when we experience inconsistencies or see a lack of equality in how others are treated. You might expect more from one staff member because they've worked with you for a long time and are usually a safe pair of hands but is that fair? Can they not have a bad day like everyone else?

## Task

Think about the standards of performance and behaviour you apply to your staff members. Are they equitable? Do you expect the same from each person or are there inconsistencies in your expectations? Do not overlook your engaged and performing staff, they need a 'well done' and a 'thank you' too.

As an employer or line manager you have a responsibility to make time available to staff to discuss their performance and behaviour, and to help resolve operational issues. How you do that is up to you. Some managers have a very open-door approach[66] and make themselves readily available to staff, while others have a more formal route of access, via a personal assistant for instance. There can be pros and cons to both approaches. An open-door approach can build a great relationship with staff but prevent you from dealing with your own work, which can lead to stress, frustration and low mood. In that situation potentially, the staff are happy and you're not. With a more formal route for staff to access your time and support you have greater control over the completion of your own work and are not facing continued, unplanned interruptions. That makes you feel happier but potentially staff are frustrated that they cannot access your time more easily. So either way, someone's not happy!

Balance is the key. If you usually leave your door open or you work in an open environment where people can access your time and interrupt you easily, find a way to balance your working day with less interruptions. That might be by moving to another workspace, closing your door for periods of time, which staff know means that you have a specific piece of work to focus on, or by using an agreed method.

Traffic light colours can be used, although people don't often take notice of those. Talk to your team and agree a way to balance your day. Explain that you do want to be on hand to deal with their queries but also need time to focus on your own work. If you can agree a solution with the team, you can hold each other to account quite easily if staff ignore the signs to indicate you're not available. You might say "oh, sorry Stephen, we did agree that when the red sign is put up, I'm not to be interrupted". Stephen will probably come on in anyway and you can decide whether you listen to his query or direct him to someone else for help. Keep making the point though and go back to the team discussion if the agreed solution is not working. You might say "so we agreed a way that I could get some uninterrupted time but that's not working because you keep charging in when my red sign is on display! Can we think about another solution please or do I need to put a system of fines in place?!". Said with humour, you can make your point and help people to understand your frustrations.

If your preference is to keep the door closed and ask people to schedule meetings with you more formally, your connection with the team might diminish over time. Scheduling time to 'walk the floor' can be useful as well as taking a less planned approach to that. If you find yourself with ten minutes to spare, use that to go and talk to members of your team. You don't have to see everyone; while it can be useful to say 'hello' to everyone together, bear in mind you will be interrupting them at that point, so assessing the landscape and having a quick chat with staff members that you come into contact with less frequently can be a great way to show you value their efforts and is likely to support their continued engagement. Scheduling regular team meetings is also a great way to keep in touch with the team if, for some reason you aren't in the same work space as them.

Making time available to staff members can take a range of forms, to include one-to-one meetings, team meetings and performance review meetings. You will know what works for your organisation and team, but a suggested frequency for those meetings is:

- One-to-one meetings – fortnightly.

- Team meetings – monthly.

- Performance review meetings – quarterly.

If that schedule feels too onerous it's worth considering if the balance of your workload and line management responsibilities is achievable.

As an employer or line manager, you have a responsibility to make time available to your staff but also to ensure you secure your own work time as well. Staff management will almost always take up more time than you have available and so it's important to communicate assertively, manage peoples' expectations and agree ways to indicate you're not to be interrupted. It won't always work because there will always be an occasion when an issue needs to be dealt with immediately but don't let the approach taken that day become the norm. Make it clear that you will respond to urgent issues but if staff members are performing well and anticipating problems, urgent issues should be a rare occurrence.

If that's not the case, have a team meeting to talk about that specifically. You might say "I want to talk about why we keep having these last-minute issues. What is it that we're not anticipating effectively?".

Staff members have a responsibility to carry out the duties of their role, as defined in their job description. If a staff member is very experienced and effective in their work it can be useful to look for development opportunities to motivate and engage them. However, their core role must still be performed. If other managers see highly effective staff members in your team, they can sometimes be guilty of trying to poach them from you with promises of much more exciting tasks and development. This must be addressed very quickly or you risk losing your best staff members and end up spending time on recruitment when you didn't expect to have a vacancy in your team. Staff will look for opportunities to progress of course and that may well be into other roles across the organisation but by having open and honest conversations with your staff member about how they're looking to progress and develop you can take a more planned approach to them moving on, instead of them being lured away to more exciting or challenging things. Even if you agree a temporary transfer or a split of responsibilities, plans for the continuation of the duties of the core role must be in place before you lose the capacity from your team.

Staff members have a responsibility to make time for your planned one-to-one meetings, team meetings and performance review meetings. Being too busy to ever attend your planned team meeting is unacceptable. Missing meetings occasionally, with given notice and agreement from you is acceptable but continued absence is not. Staff are required to engage with you and their colleagues as part of their role and a reluctance to do that must be challenged. A unilateral approach must be adopted, where attendance is required by all staff, not just by some. One rule for one person and a different set of rules for everyone else can lead to dis-engagement very quickly. If a staff member says they don't want to attend the meetings because they find them boring, ask them how they would run them or possibly ask them to lead a meeting. It's not always as easy as people think to lead meetings and generate enthusiasm so seeing the other side of that, for a reluctant attendee can give them a fresh perspective on what you're trying to achieve. Ask the team how they would like the team meetings to run. You might not be able to factor in all of their requests but by showing your consideration for the suggestions made, you show you respect and value the feedback given to you.

If you have staff members who work part-time hours try to schedule your team meetings to ensure as many as possible are included regularly and vary the days to make sure everyone can attend at some point. If most meetings are held on a day when a specific staff member is not in work, ask another member of the team to update them on what was discussed and if possible, give them advanced notice of the content of future meetings to give them an opportunity to offer their feedback on specific issues ahead of the meeting.

While you, as an employer or line manager will need to provide specific evidence if you're tackling a performance or behavioural problem, it's for the staff member to provide evidence at their performance review meetings. There is great variation across organisations as to how performance reviews are completed but as a line manager you're not responsible for collating evidence in support of performance objectives, that is the responsibility of the staff member. You might offer supplementary evidence but the responsibility to collect evidence does not primarily sit with you. As part of their working day, staff members can keep emails and records which pertain to their performance review. By doing so, it keeps their performance objectives in their minds which is important. As you set and agree performance objectives you can discuss how evidence can be given in support of achieving the objective. If that's not possible the objective will need to be re-worded. We'll focus on that in chapter 12.

Staff members have a responsibility to make time available to talk to you and to take part in team meetings. They must also engage with you to discuss issues, identify possible solutions and areas for change, and agree a way forward. If a staff member is not prepared to engage with you, is not willing to recognise a problem or identify areas for change, more formal action will be required. Most people will respond well to feedback, if given constructively, kindly and compassionately but some will have no intention of making changes and will see your feedback and subsequent actions as a challenge to fight. Some people like a fight and enjoy the conflict and disruption they can create, which can also delay finding a solution and test your tenacity and resilience to continue with your challenge to their performance or behaviour. More formal measures need to be put in place very quickly if you experience an aggressive reaction from a staff member when you challenge them.

## Signposting to Support

It's important that you have an awareness of the organisational policies and the support available to you and your staff members before you enter into a difficult conversation.

Support can include:
- signposting to HR colleagues for support and advice.

- referrals to Occupational Health teams.

- details of private health care, wellbeing or counselling services which your organisation commission to support staff members.

- details of disciplinary or capability procedures, your leave policy or mediation services for instance.

It's not always possible to predict how a difficult conversation will progress so a willingness to identify options for specific support can also be important. During a conversation, a staff member might confirm that they have recently taken on caring responsibilities for a family member or friend for instance, so finding the details of a local carer's organisation is helpful. Yes, the staff member could do that themselves but if they're struggling to cope, you can show your support and commitment to their continued wellbeing by offering to identify options for support for them. That approach can secure the continued engagement of the staff member during difficult times and beyond, and that can help to sustain your organisational strength and resilience.

## Monitoring Progress

Once a difficult conversation has taken place it's important that progress is monitored and you continue to check in with the staff member, either to confirm the required changes are being seen or that progress is not being made as you expected. Leaving a difficult conversation without an agreed way forward undermines the whole process and the effort it's taken for you to address the issue in the first place. Agreeing next steps and the defined requirements for change at the end of a difficult conversation is a must, as is an agreement on when you will next meet to discuss the situation. You will judge the interval before progress is to be monitored, in line with the issue itself and the individual staff member but a week is a good timescale for the first check in on progress, with a fortnight's time a maximum. Progress monitoring can be completed during planned one-to-one meetings but take care that you split the meeting, to discuss the specific issue and progress being made, as well as the general one-to-one focus of where things are up to.

It can be useful to use a planned performance review meeting as a sign off that no further progress monitoring is required, if the required improvements are seen. You might say "we'll meet up regularly to review progress and then spend some time in your next quarterly performance review to confirm if things are where they need to be". That approach shows the staff member that the issue is being taken seriously and that a reasonably formal approach, of a conversation during the performance review, is being taken. Depending on the issue being addressed, you can also use future performance review meetings to check in on progress particularly if the issue relates to a less frequent task, such as the development of a quarterly or end of year report.

Making written notes and keeping an audit trail of progress can be useful but might depend on the issue to be addressed. Performance issues are easier to quantify than behavioural ones and so specific requirements for improvement are easier to define. In addressing a behavioural issue, it's useful to summarise your discussions during the progress monitoring meeting in an email afterwards to ensure both parties have a record of progress or a written requirement that further improvement is necessary. If improvements are noted, record that, especially if they're seen more quickly than expected. That evidence can be useful for your performance review meetings.

**Case Study**
Let's return to Susan, our staff member who is not performing well and who, up until now hasn't recognised the issue regarding her performance as a problem. In chapter 6 we focused on creating an appropriate environment for a difficult conversation and considered how verbal communication styles, body language and tone can influence the outcome of a conversation. Now we will develop a plan of action to address Susan's performance issue and her lack of awareness of the problem. The conversation between Susan and her line manager might sound something like this.

**Line manager (LM)  Susan (S)**

**LM**         "Susan, we met last week and I explained that missing deadlines for our major customers is not acceptable. Have you thought about what we discussed?"

**S**          "Yes, I've had a think about it but I really do think you're making more of an issue of it than is necessary."

**LM**         "OK. I went to see Customer A and Customer B last week and they explained that they're both looking for new providers as we keep missing the delivery deadlines. That's part of your role, to make sure the end product reaches them on time. Are you experiencing delays, with the different parts of the service being delivered to you?"

S    "Sometimes there are delays from other departments and  then I struggle to collate everything but that doesn't happen very often."

LM    "How confident do you feel about collating the different aspects of the service?  Is it hard to do that for lots of customers when there are time pressures?"

S    "It can be difficult and sometimes I struggle to use the new software that you brought in but no one's ever complained, so I didn't really think it was a problem."

LM    "It is a problem, we have two major customers looking for new providers so we do need to get to the bottom of this.  Other members of the team have taken calls when customers A and B haven't been happy, have you not seen those messages?"

S    "I did but I thought I should just hurry up and get the service to them, instead of dwelling on the complaint."

LM    "Can you talk me through how you plan your work to meet the different customer deadlines?"

S    Susan explains the way she prioritises her work and her approach seems very organised.

LM    "You mentioned that you struggle with the new software, can you talk to me about that please?"

S    Susan explains that she was on leave the week the software was introduced and then just received a quick overview from her colleague, Mike when she returned to work. She feels she should be doing better with it than she is but doesn't like to bother the rest of team to ask for help.

**LM** "Would it be helpful if I arranged for the software trainer to come back in to do a training session for you and some of the other staff who've joined the team since the initial training was completed?"

**S** "That would be great, are there other people who are struggling with it as well then?"

**LM** "I haven't asked them specifically to be honest but if you're struggling because you missed the initial training, then it stands to reason that others will be too."

**S** "It might just be because I'm not so great with new technology."

**LM** "It doesn't really matter either way Susan, I didn't focus on who'd had the training after that first week, so it'd be good to get the software team back again to do some training and refresher sessions for the team."

**S** "OK, thanks, that'll be useful."

**LM** "When we first spoke, you said it wasn't a problem that the deadlines were being missed but that is a problem. Can you see how customers will be affected by that?"

**S** "I've never really thought about it, I just thought that the odd day's delay wouldn't really matter."

**LM** "But there have been complaints from Customer A and Customer B. Did that not make you think that it was important to deliver against the deadlines?"

**S** "I just thought they were being grumpy."

**LM**  "I think they were being grumpy because any delays from us cause delays in other parts of their organisation, which has a knock effect to their customers.  They were getting complaints as well but that was because you were missing your deadlines.  They said they had raised it with your previous line manager, did he not talk to you about that?"

**S**  "No, he didn't say anything about it."

**LM**  "OK, so what I think we should do is arrange for you and I to go and see Customers A and B in a few month's time so we can understand the impact of us missing deadlines.  It'll also be good to meet and get to know them a bit more, to build our relationships with them.  That way, if there are issues, they'll hopefully feel more comfortable to ring one of us to ask for an update on progress and to explain the impact of delays.  It's important that you meet the deadlines on all the services so if you're struggling, book some time with me and we can talk about what's making that difficult.  I'll arrange for the software company to come back in and we'll set up a training session and some one-to-one support, to make sure you feel comfortable with the system.  In the meantime, are you on course to meet your current deadlines or are you struggling with some of them?"

**S**  "I've got two that I've not been able to log as I can't seem to access the right screen on the system but I thought I'd have another go at that this afternoon."

**LM**  "How about I ask Lindsey to come and sit with you later for half-an-hour to see if you can sort that out together?  She seems to be able to whiz around that system faster than  any of us."

**S**  "That'd be great, thanks.  I didn't want to ask

Lindsey,
because I can see she's always so busy."

**LM**        "She is, but she's happy to help other people if she can. Sometimes it's just about asking her for help and then letting her find a time when you can sit down together."

**S**        "OK."

**LM**        "I'll try to get the software training session set up for about two week's time but let's sit down before that to check in on progress and to reflect on what we've discussed today. I'll book us some time for the end of next week but please let me know if you think those two orders are going to miss their deadlines, as I can get a couple of other staff members to pitch in if they need to, to make sure we deliver on time. It's really important that we hit all the deadlines now and build our relationships with Customer A and Customer B, to show them that we're an effective provider. Is there anything else you'd like to talk about today Susan?"

**S**        "No, thanks. I'm glad we had this chat, I didn't realise that Customers A and B were looking elsewhere and that I'm playing a part in that. I'll try to make sure that all the deadlines are met in future and will let you know if I'm struggling to make that happen."

**LM**        "Thanks Susan. I'll go and talk to Lindsey now, to arrange for her to spend some time with you this afternoon."

By exploring the range of issues affecting Susan's performance and assertively explaining that there is a problem when she misses deadlines, the difficult conversation can be negotiated with a friendly style. Susan has clearly been ignoring messages and feedback from the team that her customers are not happy, so it could be useful to add an objective into her next performance review, to develop a process to gauge customer satisfaction levels for all of the teams' customers, not just her own, and to work with the rest of the team to develop it. That will help Susan to build relationships with her colleagues, which will make it easier for her to ask for help if she needs it, and will raise her awareness of how other team members work effectively with their customers.

Consensus can influence performance and behaviours as people will look to the actions and behaviours of others to determine their own standards. Spending time with colleagues will give Susan a more informed sense of her line manager's and the team's expectation of what standard of performance is required in terms of meeting customer deadlines.

After reading this chapter, think about how you manage difficult conversations and if you have the right information with you to anticipate some of the issues that might come up. You can't account for every direction the conversation will take but by using a friendly, supportive and assertive approach you can manage the conversation more easily, influence the outcome effectively and maintain a high level of credibility. If you can't answer a question in relation to an organisational policy, direct the staff member to where they can find the document and ask them to confirm the details to you. While it can be helpful if you can confirm the information, if you receive a less usual request it's appropriate for the staff member to take some time to find out about the organisational policy themselves to inform a further conversation between you.

How well do you monitor progress in relation to improved performance and behaviour? Do you hope the problem will go away once you've addressed it? While a problem might go away in the short term following your conversation to address it, if the staff member is not seeing a level of progress monitoring, they may well revert back to lower performance or standards of behaviour very quickly. They may think that your conversation was a one-off because you were having a bad day and slowly relax their standards again. Line management is relentless but if you demonstrate consistency and ensure standards of performance and behaviour are where you want them to be, things do get easier. But it does take time, energy and resilience to embed effective changes.

# Chapter 9

# Agreeing a Way Forward

For many years medical professionals have tried to tell people how to lose weight, stop smoking and take more exercise. Patients have been shown pictures of plates of food, with proportions of vegetables, proteins and carbohydrates on them on many occasions in an attempt to make them think more consciously about their eating habits and to promote a healthier lifestyle. Does the picture of the plate make a difference in many of those cases? No, because the answers are with the individual, as to how they will adopt a healthier lifestyle and possibly lose weight. In the same way, the answers are with your staff if there are issues with their performance, behaviour or attendance.

As a line manager, you will:

*   listen and offer support.

*   make suggestions for change.

*   define policies and processes.

*   monitor progress.

*   signpost staff members to additional support options.

Ultimately the responsibility to change is with the individual. We can help to create an environment conducive to change but the choice to make changes is with them, not you.

**The Answers are With Them**
To give an example of an effective solution, in some areas the NHS has delivered motivational interviewing training to healthcare professionals. In healthcare, motivational interviewing changes the traditional approach of giving patients lots of information about why they should lose weight, stop smoking and exercise more, which typically they would nod along to during

their appointment but not buy into as a way of life. A motivational interviewing approach is one that asks the patient, client or staff member why and how they will make a change. By supporting a patient to find their own motivation and solutions they're much more likely to be invested in those solutions and embed changed behaviours into their lives. It might not always work but it's a great way to start a conversation.

**Example**
A Practice Nurse has a conversation with an older lady, Mary about her high blood pressure and needs to suggest that her weight is likely to be a factor in that. The Nurse uses the evidence of the blood pressure results and asks "how's life been for the last few months Mary, are you feeling fit and healthy?". Mary tells the Nurse that's she's not been getting out much recently and has struggled to climb the stairs in the last few months. The Nurse then asks "what can you do to make changes do you think?". There the issue of needing to lose some weight is identified, but it's identified by Mary and not by the Nurse which is important. The Nurse asks "how do you think you can do that, how can you be more active?". Mary tells the Nurse how she used to enjoy going out for walks with her grandchildren but they don't do that so much now as they're older. Her friend, Jenny has a dog and often invites Mary out to walk with them but she hasn't taken up the invitation, so maybe she will do that now.

Mary leaves her appointment with the Nurse feeling more empowered to act. She has re-connected with things that she enjoys and is much more likely at that point to motivate herself to make change happen. With regular check-ins to help Mary see her progress, to re-motivate her again or to talk about why she's not making the progress she hoped for, the responsibility and motivation stays with Mary. The Nurse is the facilitator of those conversations, guiding Mary to find her own motivation and energy, and move towards a more positive cycle of behaviour that will make Mary feel much better and will also very likely reduce her blood pressure, which was the original aim.

We can all get stuck and sometimes a facilitated conversation is what we need to help us find our own solutions which will motivate us to act. There are lots of solution[67] and outcome-based therapy models, motivational interviewing is just one of them. The most important aspect of those models is the fact that the responsibility stays with the individual and that can translate very effectively into the workplace. There can sometimes be a fear, particularly in Health that there won't be enough time to have those sorts of conversations, that there's only enough time to push information at a patient, not to let them explore their own solutions. But with practice those conversations don't actually need to take very long at all. Having faith in your own ability can sometimes be a barrier to making change and embracing a new approach.

Generally, people are not looking to perform poorly so if you do have a staff member who is not performing, behaving or attending as you would expect, you will need to talk to them. By using open questions, you can start the conversation with the staff members' thoughts and go from there. It can be tempting to launch into "well this isn't good enough!" but keep in mind that there's usually a reason why there's a problem and if you keep the conversation with the staff member calm, you're much more likely to find an underlying reason for the issues and manage to agree a way forward.

There are so many versions of this conversation that it would be impossible to consider them all here but let's have a look at three possible situations.

- There's a problem with a staff members' work performance but they think things are fine.

You start your conversation by asking "how do you think things are going?" and the staff member, John says he thinks things are going well. You then ask "how do you feel about the balance of your work responsibilities, are they achievable?". This will hopefully lead the conversation into areas about where he's doing well and not so well. If he continues to say everything's fine you will need to say something like "there are some aspects of your work that are not where they need to be. I'd like to talk about that" and that's where you use specific evidence of what and why John's work isn't at an acceptable level in some areas. It might be that he's not realised the impact of less accurate information, for instance and by explaining that, you allow him to see the effect his actions have on other people, which will hopefully be enough to motivate him to change. At that point you can agree how you will monitor the situation and check in again to review progress. You must follow up, otherwise the impact of the conversation can be lost and that's not productive when you've made the effort to tackle the issue in the first place. That would be a waste of your energy.

•      There's a problem with a staff members' behaviour but they perform very well.

It can be challenging to tackle a staff member's behaviour when their expertise and work performance are key to the delivery of your business but to retain the respect of your other staff it must be tackled. Inconsistencies in how you allow people to behave will undermine your influence if you try to tackle problems elsewhere in the organisation. Staff see what is happening in other departments, they talk about it and observe your responses, so if you allow someone's poor behaviour to go unchallenged that will create problems for you in the future.

The conversation with staff member Emma can start in the same way as before "how do you think things are going?". You might use that opportunity to talk about recent successes and Emma's part in them. You could then ask "how do you think your relationships are with the rest of the team?" and that might start to tease out any difficulties. Ultimately you might have to clarify the situation with a comment such as "I've noticed your behaviours with Nick recently and we need to talk about that. How do you think your relationship is?". You will need specific evidence of what you deem to be unacceptable, to explain why the behaviour is unacceptable and what behaviours you do expect to see from Emma. It might also be useful to ask "is anything happening that's making you behave differently?" and that can encourage Emma to open up about a problem outside of work, for instance or to indicate that she's feeling frustrated that she's stuck in her role, with no sign of development and is frustrated with the level of dependency on her. She might feel overwhelmed by that so it's useful to talk about how other staff can cover different aspects of her role.

Again, you will need to confirm how you will monitor the situation and make plans to check in again to discuss progress. With a supportive approach, a conversation which starts as a challenging one can end with the staff member feeling relieved to have discussed their frustrations, grateful that you've taken the time to talk to them and reassured that you have noticed the change in their behaviour. That shows you care, that you will challenge unacceptable behaviours and have a supportive conversation to understand what the reasons for that might be.

- A staff member repeatedly calls in sick but avoids your meetings to discuss their absence.
  Their work performance is good when they're in work.

Sickness absence can result in a formal organisational response quite quickly, particularly if you have absence triggers which generate alerts to line managers but if you can have an informal conversation with a staff member before the alert stage, that's useful for a number of reasons. It might be that the staff member has a progressively worsening illness but is struggling to come to terms with that, and that definitely needs a conversation, particularly to signpost them to possible forms of current and future support. The staff member may have significantly more caring responsibilities suddenly, which you've not been made aware of and it's important to discuss that too.

Your conversation with staff member Fiona can start with a question such as "how are things with you?". That might be enough to motivate Fiona to tell you about what's happening but if not, you might say "could you talk to me about your recent absences? I'd like to understand if there's any support we can offer you to help". If Fiona takes the opportunity to talk about her situation at that point the conversation can progress to ensure she is engaged with her G.P. (USA = M.D.) and other health services if that's applicable and to re-affirm your absence policies. You can also confirm that Fiona needs to make sure she attends meetings to discuss her absences as it's essential that you, as her manager or employer demonstrate a duty of care towards her. You want to make sure she's OK and that she's fit to work effectively and if that's not the case you need to have ongoing conversations to talk about that.

If Fiona chooses not to be honest about her situation it may be that there are more general work issues which are affecting her willingness to come into work. A question such as "how are things going here?" might help to draw out any performance or behaviour issues, either with Fiona or from other staff members that are affecting her willingness to come into work.

It's important that you clarify what you expect from Fiona, that you make plans for a follow up meeting and that she is clear about your formal absence policy. It's also important to explain the support that is available to her and the need for her to engage with health and support services as applicable. Together you can usually work through even the most difficult of situations but if she is not honest with you then that will be more difficult. Sometimes staff can be reluctant to talk about deteriorating health issues or increasing carer responsibilities as they're worried about their financial security. They may well need their full-time salary but are unable to consistently work full time hours, for various reasons and so their increasing absence is a way of avoiding a conversation which admits their difficulties. While you must be sympathetic to their situation you must also represent the organisation. You cannot pay staff for work they're not doing long-term but with ongoing, supportive conversations and signposting to additional forms of support you can find a way forward for the staff member and the organisation. Those conversations are not easy but difficult situations do need to be acknowledged and dealt with effectively. They will not miraculously disappear if you don't address them.

Be mindful of the questions you use to start a conversation. "How are things?" is a general question and may get a very high-level response. "How do you think things are going?" is looking for a more specific response as to how the staff member feels things are and that can be a good way to start a conversation in which you're looking to address a performance or behavioural issue. You'll develop your own style of course, so think about what works well and keep using the effective techniques and approaches you identify.

## Coaching Techniques

There are a range of coaching techniques available, many of which can be accessed online but the key principles are based on active listening and great questioning techniques which we focus on in this chapter. Chapters 6, 7 and 8 focus in more detail on difficult conversations and influencing change and appendix B of this book includes details of specific questioning techniques.

## Active Listening
## Task

Think about a time when someone didn't listen to you, didn't hear what you were saying or didn't allow you to put your point across?  How did that feel?

Listening actively to someone can be a gift and can often be all you need to do, to allow someone to air their views, worries or difficulties and give them the time and space to find their own solutions.  Not actively listening to someone when you've asked to talk to them about an issue is unproductive, ineffective and pretty much a waste of time for both of you.  The conversation initially is about them, not you.  It's about what they have to say and how they think things are going.  If you wade in with talk of how your day is going, how difficult things are for you, you can dis-engage people very quickly.  It's good to have a brief informal discussion before a conversation about a problem starts but be very clear, when that conversation starts, it's about them and not you.  If you're struggling for some reason, are feeling under pressure or are struggling to meet deadlines you need to talk to your line manager about that, not your member of staff.

It can be difficult to find the right balance to your approach, especially if you've built close relationships and friendships with your team members over a period of time but there's nothing wrong with saying something like "OK, so we need to talk about something specific today" to indicate that the less formal conversation is over.  That might lead into the question "how do you think things are going?".  You've made it clear that there is a specific reason for your conversation, it's not just a catch up, general conversation.  It can be good to have a general catch up conversation sometimes but you will both benefit if there are some fixed expectations of what will come out of that conversation, such as an agreed way forward.

What does active listening look like?  Sometimes it can be easier to focus on what it doesn't look like first.

Ineffective listening can look like:

• Looking away from the person while they're talking.

- Looking beyond them, to someone else moving around in the office.

- Looking at your watch.

- Checking your phone, particularly if it pings with a text or email.

- Fidgeting.

- Reading something while a person is talking.

- Closed and distracted body language.

- Doodling.

- Looking out of the window.

- Yawning.

- Showing no signs of understanding, such as nodding or giving verbal cues.

You will know how some of those situations feel. It's not good is it? Think about your behaviours when you listen to people. Often your physical gestures can become very embedded and you become less conscious of them but if you're looking to challenge a staff member about their performance or behaviour it's vital that you actively listen to what they're saying. If you're challenging a behavioural problem, in particular it's important that you demonstrate effective behaviours yourself. Otherwise someone might challenge you on it and that can undermine your credibility.

What does active listening look like? The following points will help you make the right impression:

- Good eye contact – people don't always feel comfortable with continued eye contact but make sure you make eye contact regularly to show you're actively listening to what the other person is saying.

- If possible, sit with your body facing towards the other person or make sure you're looking towards them at least. Looking at the side of someone's head doesn't give the impression that you're being listened to.

- Nod or usual verbal cues to confirm your understanding. "Yes", "I see" or "I understand" for instance.

- Reflect back or summarise. Coaching techniques suggest that reflecting back what someone has told you or summarising the content of what they've said can be very useful in showing that you've understood the context and content of the conversation.

- Sit forward to indicate you're actively interested in what the other person is saying. Staying slumped in your chair sends a strong message of dis-interest.

- Stay still, don't fidget or look at your laptop screen unless it's relevant. You might say "just let me check the dates of when those reports are due" to indicate that you need to access additional information but don't then read two emails that have just come in at the same time!

- Pay attention! If you're doodling or checking the time continuously, your mind is elsewhere. An effective conservation can take much less time if you pay attention and listen actively from the outset. Otherwise you may well be asking for clarification on something that's already been said and that shows that you weren't actively listening in the first place.

- Keep your body language open. People can get hung up on the body language meaning of crossing your arms when many people actually do that because it's comfortable to sit in that position. It can also help us to stop fidgeting if that's a problem. If you do cross your arms but are still looking towards the other person, are maintaining eye contact with them and are sitting forward, you're still engaged and actively listening to what they're saying. Crossing your arms, sitting back and looking away is definitely a sign of being dis-engaged, uninterested and not valuing what the other person is saying.

- Listen completely to what's being said before planning your response. To some extent our brains will always be planning our responses during a conversation but if you make notes of any important points that you don't want to miss, you can listen actively and objectively to what's being said. This does take practice but if your time is spent thinking about your responses to what's being said, you're not actively listening any more and the conversation has gone back to being about you. While the other person is talking, the conversation is not about you, it's about them. Once the other person has finished speaking you could say "that's really helpful, thank you. Let me just check through my notes before I respond to the points you've made".
Taking a moment before you reply shows that the conversation has been taken seriously and the points raised have been heard. It also gives you time to structure your response and prioritise the issues which can be important, particularly if a number of issues have been raised.

- Don't be distracted by other colleagues, visitors or events going on around you. Hopefully your conversation will take place in a meeting room or private office, so distractions will be kept to a minimum but other staff may well look into the room if they're trying to find a venue for their meeting so try to position yourself in the room so that you're not distracted by faces at the door.

**Open Questions**
As you'll already know, an open question[68] is one that cannot be answered directly by a 'yes' or 'no' answer, it requires a more detailed response. And while some people are highly skilled at shutting down even the most open of questions, using them will help you to draw out more detailed responses, particularly when you're discussing difficulties and problems.
If you ask, "how do you think things are going?" and the

reply is "fine", it's acceptable to say something like "could you expand on that for me? What's working well, and not so well for you at the moment?". If barriers are still being put up it might be necessary to move onto what you want to talk about more quickly than you would like, but if that gets the conversation to progress it might be your only way forward.

Open questions are designed to explore someone's thoughts, to make them do the thinking and to talk about their situation, and sometimes their emotions and fears. If a staff member is finding something difficult or is avoiding an issue, they may continue to shut down your open questions. Stick with it. If there's an issue that's affecting a staff member's performance or behaviour there is a requirement for them to talk to you about it, the possible reasons why the situation has occurred and to engage in a conversation with you to make things improve[69]. If this approach is new to them, they may believe that a continued lack of engagement will let them off the hook and so your tenacity, determination, kindness and compassion will be key to making the staff member feel secure enough to reveal their vulnerabilities.

You might say something like "you don't seem to be as happy in your role at the moment. Could you talk to me about that?", and then focus on the different aspects of their work to check if things are OK with each of them. For example, you might ask if things are OK generally in the work environment and ask if their working relationships are effective. "Is there anyone you're finding it difficult to work with?" can be an effective question. It's a more closed question but as you talk about the details of a situation you can use more closed questions to tease out the specifics of an issue. Open questions are effective to get the conversation started.

**Appendix B** includes details of the TGROW model which gives a great structure for a coaching conversation. TGROW stands for Topic, Goal, Reality, Options and Way forward and that can be a great tool to take with you if you're unsure as to how a conversation will progress. It can also help you stay on track if conversations are wandering and moving into a general moan about how things are. You might say "so, we've talked about the reality of what's happening for you but now let's look at the options available to us, to make things change".

Appendix B also details some challenging questions which are great for re-directing a conversation into a more positive focus. A popular challenging question is "who else is losing sleep over this?" because sometimes staff members will worry about situations for which they're not accountable.  They see potential issues on the horizon and might struggle to escalate their concerns.  Or their worry might stem from not knowing the more strategic landscape, which allows you to know that a potential issue will not cause significant problems because other events will reduce its impact.  You might not be in a position to tell your staff member about more strategic plans but the question of 'who else is losing sleep…' can offer an opportunity for reassurance that things are in hand, are being dealt with and are not a major cause for concern for you, the person who is ultimately accountable.

There are three ways to deliver strategic plans, particularly if they will affect a period of change for your team or organisation. The third option is an important one, that leaders often fail to utilise.

1.  "I know what the plans are and I can tell you about them".

2.  "I don't know what the plans are but I will tell you as soon as I know".

3.  "I do know what the plans are but I can't tell you yet.  I do expect to be able to confirm the details (in two weeks, for instance)".

If your organisation is psychologically safe, you will have built a level of trust which reassures people that you will tell them about strategic changes as soon as you can.  If your organisation is about to embark on a significant period of change, there will be many factors that will influence when details can be given out, such as the impact of those changes will have on specific parts of the workforce.  Two great open questions for one-to-one or team meetings are:

•  "what do you think about the planned changes?"

• "how do you feel about what's been proposed?"

These questions give staff an opportunity to air their concerns, many of which can be expected to be about their financial security and potentially changed job roles. While you might be concerned about significant strategic changes and how you and your team will work through the period of transition over the next two years, your team members are likely to be more concerned about their job security, their commute distance and how their job might change. It's normal for them to be concerned about those things, it's part of our psyche to be concerned about the smaller details of change. In times of change and transition, we'll all think 'what does that mean for me?'. While you might find it frustrating, being asked about the minutiae of what the change will mean for you as a team

## In times of change and transition, we'll all think 'what does that mean for me?

and for your team members as individuals, particularly as you may well not have the answers to those questions, it's important that you acknowledge people's concerns and reassure them. Often the end result of significant strategic change is not clear when you first embark on it, particularly in terms of the finer details of where everyone will sit and how job roles might change but staff will feel reassured if you continue to have conversations with them about what's happening. Sometimes, as leaders we have to say "I don't know yet" but it's better to do that, than not have a conversation with your teams when they have concerns about how they will be affected.

**Empathy and Rapport**
**Task**

Think about how you would like to be treated if you were experiencing problems at work. What would work well for you and what wouldn't?

Sympathy can be defined as:
  *feelings of pity and sorrow for someone else's misfortune.*

It might sound like *"ah, poor you"*.

Empathy is defined as:
> *the ability to understand and share the feelings of another.*

It might sound like:
> *"I can see why you're upset"*.

**Sympathy** can also be defined as a shared feeling between two people but the important factor is to not pity the other person. Very few people want you to feel sorry for them, it's part of their feelings of self-respect so it's important to show that you're trying to understand how someone feels, even if that wouldn't be a significant issue for you. If we return to the scenario of a staff member being upset because their pet has died, it doesn't matter how you would feel in that situation, it's important to try and understand the other person's feelings of loss and bereavement, and to offer support during a difficult time.

**Empathy**[70] demonstrates your understanding of someone's feelings about a situation, whether you agree with them or not. You might have a member of staff who feels they're being bullied for instance but you don't think that's the case. In the first instance, it's important to listen to why they think they're being treated unfairly as you might not know the full details of the situation. Once you do know the full details of the situation it's still not for you to decide whether you think the staff member is right or wrong, their reality and the impact of it is what's important. An empathetic conversation will help you both to move forward more quickly than time spent disagreeing on whether the staff member is being bullied or not. Their reality is key and that's what you need to work on. The following statements can be useful:

- "I can see you're upset about what's happening".

- "This is obviously making you feel anxious".

- "There's clearly been an impact on you".

If the staff member asks if you agree with them, in terms of their view of events, it's important to give a neutral response. You could say "my views are not important, it's the impact on you that we need to focus on".

As with active listening, empathy can be a gift to someone when they're struggling. Showing that you understand why someone is upset, anxious, angry or disappointed doesn't mean that you agree with their response, it means you can put yourself in their shoes and understand why they feel the way they do. You're not validating their emotions and agreeing that yes, for instance, they're being bullied. You're confirming your understanding of how they're being affected by a situation and looking to help them work through it.

If you do agree with your staff member that the treatment they're experiencing is unacceptable, that can make the conversation more difficult as you will often draw on your own experiences and show empathy by sharing experiences. That can be very dangerous as you might inadvertently support a case further down the line with your comments. "But you agreed with me!" your staff member might say. It's important to stay as neutral as possible and to support your staff member to work through a difficult situation, possibly while taking action outside of your discussions to manage other aspects of the situation, such as another staff member's behaviour for instance.

The body language of empathy looks very much like that of active listening and so nodding and maintaining regular eye contact will help to show you're listening well and trying to understand the impact of

> *'The body language of empathy looks very much like that of active listening.'*

a situation. Summarising and reflecting back the conversation are ways to show you have understood the content and key points of the discussion. You can also use open questions to think about the wider emotional impact of a situation, such as:

*   "how is all this is making you feel?".

---

- "how is the situation affecting you outside of work?".

- "how is the situation affecting other aspects of your work here?".

- "how do you feel about coming into work at the moment?".

- "what does your partner (significant other, family member or close friend) think you should do?".

By asking how someone feels about a situation and how they're being impacted by it in other areas of their life, you acknowledge there is an emotional impact from what's happening. That allows you to discuss the impact and move forward by offering support; either by signposting the staff member to support or by confirming the actions you will take to influence the situation. You don't need to agree with the staff member, this is about them not you, but by showing your empathy and support it's more likely that you'll be able to secure the staff member's continued engagement and commitment to their role during a difficult time. Checking in regularly is important and that can be through more formal and informal methods. A regular "how are you doing" in the office might be appropriate alongside a more formal check in once every two weeks but you'll judge that yourself, depending on the staff member and the situation.

If you ask 'how are you doing?' and the response looks to be an emotional one, try to find a more private space for a longer conversation, either at the time or later in the day. You will have a busy schedule and so it won't always be possible to 'pause' your day in order to spend time with a staff member but by saying "I've got meetings for the rest of the day but let's check in properly tomorrow, I'll find us a meeting room" you're showing your ongoing support for the staff member. And while they might prefer you to pause your day and talk to them right now, hopefully they will respect that that's not always possible.

By confirming that you'll see them the following day you're demonstrating a willingness to offer support, balanced with a need to fulfil your own work commitments. Unfortunately, while it can be very well-meaning, if you pause your day as soon as a staff member looks to be struggling, to make time to talk to them, that can create an expectation that you will always do that. It's for you to judge but it can be useful to use the 'we'll meet up later or tomorrow to discuss things' approach to demonstrate that you have work commitments too.

## Task

What does it feel like to have a good rapport with someone? Or a less positive rapport? Think about the people you have a good rapport with. What has allowed that rapport to develop?

      Good rapport is not always a tangible thing. It can be a feeling, similar to those feelings of being listened to and being dealt with empathetically but it's important that you find a level of rapport with your team members. Shared experiences can help to build rapport; liking the same sports team or TV programmes can help to do that but you don't need to have something in common with someone in order to build rapport with them. The shared goal of wanting to do a good job and support the team to succeed can be enough.

Rapport can be defined as:
*a close and harmonious relationship in which the people or groups concerned understand each other's feelings or ideas and communicate well.*

Even if you have a varied mix of people in your team, by treating each other with respect, actively listening to one another and being empathetic you can build great rapport[71].

The shared experience is the work you're doing and the challenges and successes of that can bring you together to build rapport and make you an effective unit. Team meetings[72] are a great way to build rapport, particularly if you have the courage to deviate from the usual format of everyone giving updates on their work responsibilities.

Sometimes, that's a way to avoid doing one-to-one meetings with individual staff members, by hearing their work updates collectively. Whereas if you're scheduling regular one-to-ones with staff, you can use your team meeting for other, far more interesting things than mundane work updates!

Your team meeting agenda might look something like this:

| Agenda Item | Action Required |
|---|---|
| **Team Support** – is there support anyone needs from other team members to enable them to make progress with their work? | Define the support required and sign off on actions to be taken. |
| What are our strengths? | All team members to take part in the discussion. |
| What are we not so good at? | All team members to take part in the discussion. |
| How can we work together to support each other and improve the things we're not so good at? | Discuss options and sign off on actions to be taken. |
| What would you do tomorrow if you won the lottery tonight? | All team members to take part in the discussion. |
| Confirm the details of the next meeting. ||

**Figure 5 – Proposed Team Meeting Agenda**

The agenda content will need to be varied from meeting to meeting but asking one person to talk about an interest outside of work can also help teams get to know each other well and build rapport. There needs to be a clear expectation that everyone will contribute though, even if that's just to talk about what they did with their family or friends that weekend. Equality across the meeting is important, in terms of contributions. If some team members feel their contributions are not being matched by others, they may well dis-engage from the process and contribute less. They will be looking to you to make sure that equality of effort and contribution is secured so it's important to ensure that plans are sustained and not left to dwindle if it's easier not to challenge and support a staff member who doesn't want to contribute.

What is a lack of rapport? You'll already know how that feels so be mindful of that when you talk to people, especially one-to-one. Do not try to make connections that aren't there. If you're new to a team as the line manager and are trying to get to know your staff, it can be easy to try too hard to find shared experiences or things that you have in common. Your work brings you together, hopefully along with your shared desire for great success so get to know your staff in a work capacity first, build rapport with them on that basis and then wider shared experiences and common interests will be identified.

Great rapport is unlikely to happen overnight so give yourself some time to get to know your staff, to find out more about them and to identify connections between you. Using your team meetings as a way to get to know your staff is very effective if you give them the time and space to tell you about themselves. Using questions like 'what was the first gig you went to?' is great for learning more about the interests of your team and building a great rapport with them. Raising money for charity can also be a great way to bring people together and to find out more about them.

**Defining Expectations**

Discussing a performance, behavioural or attendance issue with a staff member requires a defined expectation at the end of the conversation, in terms of what performance, behaviour or attendance is required and by when. It must be made clear that it's not acceptable to do nothing as a result of your conversation so it's important that you secure a commitment to change from the staff member. You might say "can you see how your drop in performance is affecting other people in the organisation?". These conversations can feel confrontational but clarity around what the problem is and what needs to happen to correct it, is useful in the longer term for three reasons.

- If the staff member readily accepts their drop in performance for instance and you discuss the reasons why that has happened, you will more likely secure their continued engagement. By defining your expectation for change to include a time scale, you're assertively demonstrating your authority as a line manager. When a line manager asserts their authority, with kindness and compassion, and with clear evidence as to what the problem is and how it impacts the organisation, they're more likely to secure a positive response from the staff member.

- If the staff member is resistant to your feedback and doesn't agree with you that there's a problem, despite your evidence and confirmation of the impact of the issue, you may have to adopt a more formal, disciplinary action. By defining your expectations, with a timescale you're giving clear direction on what needs to change. In the worst-case scenario, a tribunal will expect to see evidence of how the staff member's performance, behaviour or attendance has been managed. Defined expectations, sent by email following a conversation with the staff member, are a great way to demonstrate how they have been dealt with effectively and clear attempts to support an improvement have been made.

- If the staff member is willing to improve but situations exist which make an improvement more difficult, it's useful to use defined expectations as a checklist for change. You might say, "we did agree that you would issue the corrected reports by the end of the month but that hasn't happened. Can you talk to me about that please?". That gives you a start point for a further conversation as to why the staff member might be struggling to improve and how additional support might be required to help resolve situations which are impacting on progress.

**Policies and Support**

As you agree a way forward with a staff member, it's important that you have a sound knowledge of your organisational policies and the options for support that are available to your staff. While checking through policies can be time consuming, your meeting will be more effective if you go into it knowing the main points of your organisation's approach. It's impossible to know all of the details of all of your organisational policies but some research can demonstrate your professional response to dealing with a problem. Sometimes it can be useful to take specific policies into a meeting with you, to allow you to discuss the finer details as part of the meeting. Organisational policies can be open to interpretation and a line manager's discretion is often given in making a choice about how a situation is dealt with. Talking through the details of the policy with a staff member demonstrates that you're taking the issue seriously and are looking to treat them fairly, in line with the policy. It may also confirm why a certain approach cannot be taken. If, for instance a staff member asks for a change to their working hours, a flexible working policy which stipulates core hours will be useful to inform that conversation. Discussions may well continue beyond that first conversation, but you have demonstrated a fair approach by referring to the organisational policy in the first instance.

While it can be useful to have an awareness of your organisational policies before you go into a meeting with a staff member, options for support might be something that you find out afterwards, in agreement with the staff member. It's impossible to know how conversations will progress and while a general knowledge of your organisation's support options is great, you can't be expected to know all of them, so it's appropriate to confirm that you will look into the matter and update the staff member later. If, for instance a staff member explains that they're struggling financially and the worry of that situation is affecting their performance in work, you may have partner organisations that you can refer to, in order to offer support. Alternatively, you might contact the local Citizen's Advice office to ask if they can offer your staff member an appointment. Online searches can be a great aid to finding out what support services are available to you locally and you will be offering great support to the staff member if you offer to spend some time finding out what options might be available to them. You might agree that you'll both do some research and then come back together to agree a plan of action or ask your HR team to complete that work. There's no set approach as you can never anticipate what issues staff will present to you but offering support and investing time in identifying a range of options for support will most likely secure continued engagement from the staff member during difficult times and in turn, that will support your organisational strength and resilience.

After reading this chapter, think about the range of difficult conversations you have already experienced, not just in the workplace but in everyday situations as well. What did you learn from those conversations? Were there things that worked really well and should be added into your toolbox of how to manage people effectively or were there things that went very much not as you hoped and possibly should never be tried again? By reflecting on what worked well and what was less successful you can add effective tools into your line management practice. If you don't take the time to reflect, you might repeat mistakes or not use techniques that worked really well for you in the past.

It can take time and practice to embed coaching style conversations into your everyday language and line management practice so look to use the techniques in one-to-one meetings generally and then they'll be easier to access when you do have to deal with a more difficult conversation. If you wait to use the techniques, you might struggle to factor all the different elements into the conversation at the same time as dealing with a less than delighted staff member.

# Chapter 10

# Personality Type Can Make a Difference

A knowledge of the differences between introverted and extro-verted people can help you to manage your staff members and think about the most effective way to communicate with them[73]. A more extroverted staff member will typically give a sense of where they're at mood-wise very clearly but a more introverted person is less likely to do that, so you'll need to ask more spe-cific questions to gauge how they are.  For the purposes of this chapter, more extreme examples of extrovert and introvert be-haviour will be used to show the differences between the per-sonality types.  You know your staff and so the behaviours will translate across to the personality types of your staff members but will possibly be in a more diluted form than is discussed here.

Carl Jung defined the attitudes of introversion and extro-version[74], along with the decision-making functions of thinking and feeling.  The functions of sensing and intuition, and judg-ing and perceiving were also defined by Jung but these aspects of personality will not be considered in this chapter.  The com-bination of the attitudes of introversion and extroversion, with the decision-making functions of thinking and feeling are usu-ally sufficient to give a strong sense of an individual's personal-ity type and communication preferences, which will allow you to plan your approach to managing them.  It's also useful to think about your own personality type and communication prefer-ences as they will very much influence the way you manage and communicate with your team.

Let's look at the differences between extroversion and introver-sion. People with a preference towards extroversion are more likely to:

• be more sociable.

• have many friends.

• need to have people to engage with and talk to.

© 2019 Karen Warren

- crave excitement.

- take chances.

- act on the spur of the moment.

- like practical jokes and fancy-dress parties.

- like change.

- be care-free, easy-going, optimistic and like to laugh and be merry.

- be aggressive and lose their temper quickly.

- wear their hearts on their sleeve.

An extroverted person is less likely to enjoy:

- reading or studying by themselves.

- being alone.

- being constrained by rules and regulations.

An extrovert finds their energy in other people. If they have a problem, they're more likely to discuss it with a number of people before making a decision.

People with a preference towards introversion are more likely to:

- be quiet and thoughtful.

- be reliable and introspective.

- prefer books to people.

- be reserved and distant except to intimate friends.

- like to plan ahead.

- distrust the impulse of the moment and dislike surprises.

- take matters of everyday life seriously and prefer a well-ordered mode of life.

- keep their feelings under control.

- seldom show aggression.

- be pessimistic.

- place great importance on ethical standards.

An introverted person is less likely to enjoy:

- socialising in large groups.

- having their personal space being invaded by someone they don't know well.

- losing their temper.

An introvert finds their energy inside themselves. If they have a problem, they will try to work out the solution themselves and only then discuss their thoughts with close friends.

**In comparison:**

| An introverted person is: | An extroverted person is: |
|---|---|
| Energised by their inner world. | Energised by the outer world. |
| Inward. | Outgoing. |
| Quiet. | Talkative. |
| Thinks and may act. | Acts first, thinks later. |
| Values a depth of experience. | Values a breadth of experience. |
| Thinks to speak. | Speaks to think. |

None of us are just an introvert or just an extrovert, our preferences can change, sometimes in relation to our environment

© 2019 Karen Warren

and sometimes in relation to our stress levels. Some people are more extreme versions of introversion and extroversion and some people move very happily between them as they're less extreme versions of each attitude. The table below shows how our behaviours can move between introversion and extroversion.

| Introvert | Extrovert |
| --- | --- |
| Reserved | Outgoing |
| Likes to plan | Likes surprises |
| Can seem unemotional | Wears their heart on their sleeve |
| Holds frustrations in | Expresses frustrations more freely |
| Prefers order and structure | Likes spontaneity |
| Often on the edge of things | Usually in the middle of things |
| Restrained | Flamboyant |
| Cautious | Bold |
| Prefers a depth of information | Prefers a breadth of information |

**Figure 6 - Different Attitudes at Different Times**

The attitudes and decision-making functions identified by Jung give us four personality types:

- an introverted thinker.

- an extroverted thinker.

- an extroverted feeling person.

- an introverted feeling person.

We are not just one personality type; we're a mix of all four types and can change our behaviours to meet specific needs when we need to.

An extroverted feeling person is less likely to enjoy spending time alone, writing reports but they can do it, just as an introverted thinker can spend time with people and deliver presentations. It might take more energy to do those things, but they are achievable.

| **The Introverted Thinker** | **The Extroverted Thinker** |
|---|---|
| The introverted thinker needs to take time to understand why something needs to be done and to plan in detail. They will often observe situations for a long time before commenting on them, and because their views are well considered before being spoken, they can be viewed as being very wise, or pedantic!<br><br>On a positive day an introverted thinker can be deliberate, questioning and precise.<br>On a less effective day, they can be aloof, reserved and indecisive. | The extroverted thinker is task focused, driven and determined and will strive to ensure work progresses. They're good at delegating work and directing others. They can be perceived as being abrupt in their approach and overbearing in their style towards others as they're so determined to achieve.<br><br>On a positive day an extroverted thinker can be determined, strong-willed and purposeful.<br>On a less effective day, they can be aggressive, controlling and intolerant. |
| **The Introverted Feeling Person** | **The Extroverted Feeling Person** |
| The introverted feeling person is motivated by the feelings of others. They're happy if those around them are happy. Their focus will mainly be on people as opposed to tasks, and they will often be seen as the most caring, and self-less team member.<br><br>On a positive day, an introverted feeling person can be supportive, reliable and trusting.<br>On a less effective day they can be bland, reliant and stubborn | The extroverted feeling person is a great communicator who enjoys coming up with ideas, but who dislikes the application of detail in a piece of work. Once the essentials have been agreed they want to move on to the next challenge.<br><br>On a positive day, an extroverted feeling person can be sociable, dynamic and friendly.<br>On a less effective day, they can be indiscreet, flamboyant and hasty. |

**Figure 7 – Summary of Personality Types[75]**

No one is purely an extrovert or purely an introvert and while people do usually have a preference for one attitude or the other, they can change their preference, often in relation to the situation they find themselves in. A more extroverted person can push themselves to be less outgoing in a one-to-one, more difficult conversation for instance and a naturally more introverted person can be more outgoing when they're in a group of people they feel comfortable with, such as their colleagues, family or friends. A preference is just that, it doesn't mean that you can't act in a different way when the need arises, it just takes more energy to do that.

For a more extroverted person, a day working on their own to complete a number of financial returns will feel like hard work and they may well seek company later on in the day to help to re-charge their energy levels. Their preference is to work with other people and they generate energy from that, so working on their own for an extended period of time will not be their preference. But it doesn't mean they can't do it.

For a more introverted person, a day working at an engagement event, meeting customers and building relationships with people will feel tiring and they will need time to recover their energy levels afterwards. Their preference is to work alone or in smaller groups with less stimulation around them so an engagement event will not be their preferred working environment. A more introverted person may enjoy occasional days spent meeting new people but are unlikely to choose roles that require them to work in that environment regularly.

A more extroverted person finds their energy by interacting with other people, while a more introverted person loses their energy through that interaction. A more extroverted person will wake up each morning with lower energy levels and use interactions with others to build their energy during the day. That's why they can often be very talkative first thing, as they're looking to build their energy levels and are energised to socialise in the evening when their energy levels are at their highest.

A more introverted person wakes up with the energy they need for the day. Interactions deplete their energy over the course of the day and so they're likely to feel more tired and less inclined to socialise at the end of the day. A more introverted person thinks in their head and so it can be harder to know what they're thinking and they're less likely to share their thoughts.

A more extroverted person speaks to think, they think out loud so it can easier to gauge their mood and understand their thoughts. You don't need to ask a more extroverted person what they're thinking, they'll often be quite happy to tell you that before they're asked.

It can be difficult to see how introverts and extroverts can work effectively together but with your awareness and support, they can[76]. As a more extroverted person thinks out loud and a more introverted person thinks in their head, it can be hard to ensure a balance of communication in a team meeting for instance. Your more extroverted staff members are more likely to speak first and will think out loud if you ask them supplementary questions and that might mean you run out of time to listen to your more introverted staff members. Make sure everyone has a voice; draw people into the conversation if they're struggling to be heard. You might say, "Martin, we've not heard from you, what're your thoughts on the proposed changes to the team?". Introverts think very deeply so if they're not drawn into a meeting or conversation, they're likely to walk away without sharing their thoughts and ideas so make sure you take an equitable approach and ask everyone to contribute. Just because someone is quiet, it doesn't mean they have nothing to say. Sometimes they just need some help to find a space in the conversation and as their line manager you can demonstrate your support by making that happen.

**Task**
Think about your preference and those of your team to consider the balance of extroversion and introversion. Is that causing issues between staff members? Discussing the different preferences of the personality types can help to diffuse difficulties between staff members as
they can see their preferences are not wrong, they're just different.

**Thinking and Feeling**
Carl Jung defined the decision-making functions of thinking and feeling[77] and while people can move between the two functions, they will usually have a preference for one or the other. If your team has a mix of the decision-making styles, they'll naturally balance each other in how they make decisions, and influence each other and the progress of their work. However, if the team has a majority of staff members in either function,

difficulties may arise.

If the majority of staff members have a preference for thinking in their decision making, they will base their decisions on facts, evidence and information but are less likely to consider more emotional factors, which may or may not impact on your business. If a majority of staff members have a preference for feeling in their decision making, they will base their decisions on more emotive aspects and so may focus less on data and evidence to inform their decisions, which again, might have an impact on your business[78].

Making decisions purely based on facts and evidence when they impact on people can be short-sighted and a sure-fire way to alienate those people. Just because the evidence shows that it's more cost effective to re-house people in another area, it doesn't mean they will want to leave their homes of many years. Thinkers are less likely to consult with others if they feel they have the information they need to proceed and this can cause projects to fail as they near implementation, as consultation can be an afterthought and sometimes just a tick-box exercise, with the results barely considered.

Making decisions purely based on emotive factors can limit progress as people can be reluctant to embrace change and so are more likely to identify reasons as to why a project should not progress. Feeling decision-makers will often look to consult with others before making a decision and this can also delay progress. In the example of re-housing residents to another area, a feeling person may well feel constrained to proceed as they recognise the emotional impact of moving residents away from their homes of many years.

A balance of decision-making functions will enable more balanced decision making but teams with a majority of staff members in one decision-making function or the other can be prompted to think more widely with specific questions. For a majority of staff members with a thinking style of decision-making, you might say "so we know what the evidence is for doing this, but what about the impact on people? Have we talked to people to understand how they feel about the proposed changes?".

As thinkers, the group are likely to disregard this question as they view those aspects of their work to be less important, so it's vital that the need for the impact on people and the need for consultation is reiterated and it's made clear that work will not progress until those aspects of work have been completed.

With a majority of staff with a feeling style of decision-making, you might say "I know it feels like the right thing to do but what's the evidence to support this decision?". As feeling decision-makers the group are likely to disregard your question as they view the evidence and facts to be much less important than the potential impact on people. It must be reiterated that the evidence and facts to support the decision must be identified before work can proceed, to ensure the success of the project.

## Managing a Staff Member with a Preference for Extroversion

An extroverted person will generally let you know how things are going[79]. They speak to think and so their level of engagement and performance can be gauged quite easily. An extroverted thinker is determined and driven to achieve so they'll happily discuss target dates for completion and their ability to achieve those deadlines. They may, however be less focused on how effective their relationships are. An extroverted thinker can sometimes be so motivated to achieve that they do that to the detriment of others, so while they can hit deadlines well and drive work projects forward, their work relationships might not be as effective as you would like them to be.

Remember, extremes of behaviour are being used to demonstrate the differences between the personality types here so while behaviours might not be seen to the extent to which they're described, the descriptions will give a sense of the types of behaviour that can be expected.

An extroverted feeling person is less likely to enjoy being held to account to specific delivery times as their preferences are focussed towards communication and building relationships. They will often talk of their progress in terms of connections and networks, sometimes to divert you from their lack of progress with more planned aspects of their work. Most job roles are a balance of building effective working relationships and completing planned tasks and all of the personality types can struggle to find this balance if they only focus their efforts on the work aspects they prefer to do.

© 2019 Karen Warren

As extroverts speak to think, they can sometimes take over conversations, particularly with more introverted people. Team meetings are a particular area in which you can see this happen and so those meetings need to be managed carefully to ensure everyone can contribute equally. A balance of extroverts and introverts in the team can work well, as they can support their peers and stand up to each other. The introverts might tell the extroverts to "shush!" now and then and the extroverts might tell the introverts to "say what you think!". However, if you have more extroverts or more introverts in the team, that can create a more difficult dynamic and staff can feel they're outnumbered by people with a very different personality type to their own. Either way, it's for you, the line manager to make meetings and conversations effective; to motivate the introverts to speak up and manage the extroverts to ensure everyone can contribute.

In a one-to-one meeting or a difficult conversation, an extrovert can become very vocal as to how they feel or think about the perceived criticism levelled towards them and that can detract from making plans to improve. Bear in mind that extroverts speak to think and so you might need to spend more time hearing about how they feel or think before you can make a plan for defined improvements. You could consider holding a shorter, initial meeting to discuss the issue and then schedule a second meeting to define the required improvements. That will give the extroverted staff member more time to vent their frustrations before coming back to focus on what needs to happen next.

Because an extrovert speaks to think, they're not always listening well as more detailed aspects of required improvements are being discussed so it's worth following up on your meeting with an email to define the improvements which are expected and the timescales for change, or make sure that they write them down. Also ask for confirmation that the staff member accepts the defined improvements to ensure you have an audit trail of progress. Not all one-to-one meetings and difficult conversations will progress into formal action but once an event has occurred without a follow up, the audit trail is lost and is very hard to recover retrospectively. If a staff member is being taken through a formal disciplinary process for instance, they're highly unlikely to agree to sign off notes and actions from your previous meetings if they were not required to do so at the time.

An extrovert is energised by their outer world and so they can look to their outer world for answers and solutions if criticism is directed towards them. They're likely to identify a number of reasons as to why their progress was undermined but it's important to be clear about what the problem is and how it affects other people, to include colleagues, customers and suppliers. Your evidence will support your feedback to the staff member and if there are external reasons as to why their performance or behaviour has been unacceptable, those issues can be explored. It must be clear to the individual that the responsibility for the delivery of their job role is their own. If there are issues which have impacted on the performance or behaviour of the staff member, they should have been escalated to you proactively, instead of waiting until you have identified a problem. Do not allow yourself to be side-tracked if a staff member tries to convince you that the problem is with everyone else, not them. No workplace is perfect, there will always be issues that cause difficulties so be clear about what the problem is and how you expect improvements to be made.

Silence can be a great tool; it encourages people to speak, which can be useful at the start of a one-to-one meeting or difficult conversation. Knowing when to call a halt to things is also useful, otherwise how things need to change will never be discussed. Holding up a hand to indicate that enough has been said is useful. You might say "enough, we're getting stuck in the detail of what's happened and why but actually we need to look at what needs to change". People usually know when they're ranting and so they're reasonable when that's brought to a close.

While there can be a value to letting a staff member vent their feelings or thoughts for a short time, consider whether it's the best use of both of your time if that continues for an extended period. Taking a short break can be a good way to help someone to feel calmer and to progress onto discussing required improvements.

## Managing a Staff Member with a Preference for Introversion

A more introverted person is less likely to let you know how things are going[80]. You might assume that their work is progressing well and that they're not struggling because they have told you nothing to the contrary but that's not always the case. If a more introverted person isn't asked for a progress report or asked a direct question as to how they're getting on, they're much less likely to let you know about any personal or work difficulties they're having. Introverts internalise their difficulties, they look introspectively for solutions and while that can be a strength because it means they don't take up your time with queries and requests for support, it can mean that you assume things are fine when they're actually not. An introvert is only likely to seek external support once they have run out of things to try and as they can be quite resourceful, that can mean that things are in a worse state than you would like them to be, before you know there's a problem at all.

Introverts are prone to worry. An introverted thinker will worry less if their work is supported by facts, data and evidence as to why their work should progress. They're less emotional in their decision-making and so might be considered as detached and aloof to their colleagues. An introverted thinker will work easily within the constraints of policy, compliance requirements and deadlines but can sometimes get too involved in the detail of their work and so can struggle to move on to other tasks if they want to 'get to the bottom' of something or are not 100% happy with a specific element of their work. Introverted thinkers can become frustrated if they're not able to fully understand something and so being asked to move on to meet other deadlines could lead to a difficult conversation about managing a range of priorities.

An introverted feeling person is more emotional in their decision-making and so they might worry about the people around them, as well as the people impacted by their work and this can distract and disable them from making progress. Introverted feeling people have a strong sense of values and can become very stubborn if they feel their personal values or the wider values of an organisation are not being upheld. They can appear to agree on a plan of action but then do very little to follow up on it, if their values are not being supported. Introverted feeling people will support their colleagues and work contacts brilliantly but sometimes that can be to the detriment of their planned work. Consultation can be very important to an introverted feeling person, to ensure all parties are accepting of a proposed way forward and while often that can bring benefits to a project or task, sometimes that can delay progress, particularly if the timescales are challenging.

More introverted people think before they speak and can struggle to think if other people are talking around them. They can find open plan office environments difficult to work in, particularly if they have more talkative colleagues around them. If you have options available to staff, in terms of their work space it can be useful to discuss the working environment with staff members, to ask what their preferences are. More introverted staff members might be happy to complete their usual day-to-day tasks at their desks but ask to move away to a quieter environment if they have a specific task to focus on and it's useful to accommodate those requests if possible. Demonstrating an understanding of their personality type and preference for a quieter work environment can help to build your working relationship and build trust, to encourage the staff member to be open about personal or work difficulties.

A more introverted staff member might not contribute in a team meeting if other colleagues are dominating the conversation or if they're not specifically asked to contribute. Do not assume that a more introverted staff member has nothing to say, just because they don't say anything at a particular moment, such as in a team meeting. More introverted people are much more likely to reveal their thoughts in one-to-one meetings or in smaller group conversations and while it can be frustrating to need to have supplementary conversations after an agreement is thought to be made, interesting insights can be identified by a more introverted mind, which will be lost if a range of methods are not used to draw them into conversations. With a supportive team dynamic, it can be enough to ensure every staff member is asked to contribute in a team meeting to know that all opinions and suggestions for change have been sought.

An alternative solution is to contact the team ahead of the team meeting to give details of what is to be discussed and ask for feedback ahead of the meeting. That will give more introverted staff members time to consider proposals and items for discussion. Your more extroverted staff will plan to air their thoughts during the team meeting, they're unlikely to think any more about the issue until the meeting itself, which is fine. By giving the more introverted staff members a method of feedback which is non-verbal, via email for instance, they're more likely to reveal their thoughts and insights, and make suggestions for change.  This approach does take more work at first but you will move forward and make progress with the knowledge that all of the team has been offered an opportunity to respond and that will secure the continued engagement of staff members.  As this revised approach becomes more embedded into your processes and the team become more accustomed to it, another staff member can be asked to take on the role of collating feedback ahead of the meeting, if there is trust between the team members.

More introverted staff are likely to dis-engage if they're not given an opportunity to offer feedback, either via a non-verbal method or in a one-to-one or smaller group conversation.  They're deep thinkers and will spend time considering what they're asked to, so there is a value to finding a way to draw out their thoughts and engage them in a way that they feel comfortable.  Introverts tend to prefer a depth of information, whereas extroverts prefer a breadth of information and that knowledge can be very useful in different contexts.

In a one-to-one meeting, or difficult conversation with a more introverted staff member it may be difficult to engage them, to identify a problem or to discuss necessary improvements.  An introverted staff member may not say as much but they will already be turning the perceived criticism in on themselves.  An introvert will often say "it's probably my fault" and while that might be true it's important that they're not allowed to take responsibility for the failings of others as that can make them feel overloaded very quickly.  Be very specific in how you define a problem.  You might say "are there any reasons why you've not been able to …(complete the reports as expected, for instance)?".

A more introverted staff member might also give themselves a harder time than is necessary for the issue you've identified so it can be important to reiterate the impact of the issue.  If it's a serious issue, that must be said of course but if the issue is something that needs to be identified but doesn't have a huge impact on the staff member's colleagues, clients or suppliers, it's important to make that clear and encourage the staff member to have a proportionate response to the problem.  You might say "I can see you're worried but it's OK, we just need to make sure the future reports go out accurately".

If there is very little response from a more introverted staff member during a one-to-one meeting or difficult conversation, stick with it and use silence to encourage the staff member to open up and discuss the issue. You might say "how do you think things are going?". If they respond with "fine", it's acceptable to ask for more detail. You might prompt further conversation by saying "OK, but what's working well specifically and not so well?". If the staff member gives no answer to a specific question, you can prompt a response by saying "tell me what you're thinking" in a gentle and supportive way, as opposed to a challenging way.

Silence can be a great tool during conversations and particularly with a more introverted staff member as it gives them time to think and the space to speak. A less confident staff member might struggle to express themselves and the use of silence can encourage them to speak up, especially if the environment for the conversation is comfortable and your body language is perceived as being supportive to them. The only downside to the use of silence with a more introverted person is that they're often happy not to fill it and so prompts may be needed in order to move the conversation on. An introvert will often reflect on a conversation or situation and have additional insights to offer, so a follow up meeting or the offer of a follow up email from them if they do think of something else that's pertinent to the conversation will be useful.

After reading this chapter, think about your own personality type and those of your staff members. Is there an even balance of introversion, extroversion, thinking and feeling? Do you run things in line with your own preferences, as it's natural to do and not consider the other preferred styles? Talking about personality types is a great way to engage your team as the different preferences do resonate with people and can often add an element of humour to things that other people find frustrating. One staff member might say to a more introverted colleague "is that why you never say anything?!" and as long as that's said with humour and not as a criticism that's acceptable. Another staff member might say to a more extroverted colleague "is that why you never stop talking?!" and again with humour, that can be acceptable. Talking through the preferences of the four personality types can help staff members understand themselves and their colleagues more effectively. A further conversation about the strengths of the team can then help staff members see that the differences between them make the team stronger and more resilient, so there can be a great value in initiating that conversation.

*'Talking about personality types is a great way to engage your team as the different preferences do resonate with people and can often add an element of humour to things that other people find frustrating.'*

# Chapter 11

# Managing Diverse Teams

Diversity in teams is increasing and if supportive and trusting relationships are developed, that diversity can bring great benefits[81]. However, in some teams its diversity can have an undermining effect which does not support the wellbeing and productivity of your workforce. Younger people and older people view life differently; they have different skills and life experiences which influence their behaviour and all of those skills and life experiences can bring a value to your team if you can facilitate those supportive and trusting relationships[82]. It can be easy to fall into thinking 'I wish everyone worked in the same way as I do' but the truth is that they won't, either because of their age, their personality type, their cultural experiences, their previous work experiences or other factors. An open-minded approach to different people bringing different skills and experience into your team can support its strength and resilience.

It can be difficult to talk about gender and age without plunging into stereotypes but the easy answer for managing and supporting any staff member who's in any way different to you is to be respectful of who they are, what their preferences are and the value they bring to the team. There is no right and wrong in terms of expressing preferences. They might be different to yours but that doesn't mean that your preferences are right as the line manager and the staff member's preferences are wrong. They're just different. Ultimately you might agree to stick to your preference and sometimes you might need to stipulate how something is done but be wary of returning to the ways of the last millennium, when a more dictatorial style was evident in many workplaces. Being considerate and negotiating a way forward can take more time than the 'just do it!' approach but it will also grant you much greater staff engagement in most cases and that can be invaluable, particularly when you ask your teams to pitch in to resolve a difficult situation.

## Gender

Men and women are different – fact. We've evolved differently over millions of years, our brains are wired differently and

© 2019 Karen Warren **149**

so we'll work differently, generally speaking[83]. Women are more likely to work part-time[84] and so their needs in the workplace may well be different to other team members who are working full time hours. The key to managing someone of a different gender is to be respectful of their situation and to ask yourself 'is there an equality in how I'm treating this person?'. Unconscious bias[85] can sometimes creep into our decision making, particularly if we're experiencing similar difficulties. Is a line manager, who as a parent is struggling to settle their child in at a new Primary School following a move to a new town, going to be more lenient towards a staff member who is experiencing the same difficulties? Remember, you need to ask yourself "could I do this for everyone in the team?" and if the answer is "no, I couldn't possibly do that", then it's worth considering whether your decision and support is equitable or if you're feeling sorry for your staff member because their difficult situation resonates so much with your own experiences.

Just as different personality types can bring a diversity to the team dynamic, so can differences in gender and age. As with the personality types, a majority of one gender can create difficulties so it's important to have conversations about that, either on a one-to-one basis, with the person or people who are in the minority or more widely in a team meeting. The question 'do we recognise each other's strengths and support each other well?' might be useful as a team meeting topic, to bring in aspects of personality type, gender and age. Being in the minority group can mean that suggestions and feedback can be belittled by staff members in the majority group and it's important that as the line manager you stop those behaviours very quickly. You might say "all our suggestions are valid, just because they're different to yours, doesn't mean we should disregard them".

A male colleague was once told "you need to think more like a woman" which was probably said because the staff member wasn't getting their own way! It can be easy for gender groups to stick together and roll their eyes at the minority group to show their input is merely tolerated and not embraced or welcomed. Those behaviours belong in the last millennium and should be called out very quickly. As a line manager, you should not be complicit in those behaviours, even if you're thinking them!

As a line manager managing someone of the opposite gender, a respectful approach will almost always win out. If a staff member says "you don't understand because you're a (man or woman)" it's appropriate to point out that organisational policies are very rarely developed with specific genders in mind and the fair and reasonable application of those policies is part of your role. You do not have to be the same gender as your staff member to show empathy towards their situation and equally they should not use their gender as a reason to request additional support or lenience in the application of your organisational policies. Some roles are gender-specific of course but if policies are applied consistently across the team, there should be no grounds for complaint. Sometimes people will use a range of factors to sway your decision but that can be about them wanting to get their own way, not about their concerns for unfair treatment. With an equitable approach you can negotiate challenges to show consistent decision-making across the team.

Should women and men be treated differently? No. People should be treated in response to their own situation. Gender can influence that, if for instance a woman is more likely to have carer responsibilities for an elderly parent but an equitable approach will give consistency if a male staff member finds himself in the same situation. The issue there is around a staff member having caring responsibilities, not whether a man or a woman is taking on that role.

Is a male parent, with primary caring responsibilities for his children given more flexibility than his female colleagues? It's a challenge for a line manager to not allow their perception of a situation to influence them, to treat one staff member more favourably than another, so keep the thought 'could I do this for everyone?' at the forefront of your mind when responding to requests for support. Staff members can be very vigilant about the support and flexibility given to their colleagues and while a line manager doesn't need to justify their decisions individually, your judgement might be questioned if there are clear inconsistencies in your approach.

Is it harder for a man to line manage a woman, particularly if she becomes upset? Some men would say yes for sure! While women are more likely to show their upset, disappointment, anger or frustration more emotionally, men are more likely to hide their emotions, so both can be difficult to manage if a situation becomes heightened. The key is to give people time to express their emotions, to listen and to move the conversation on to discussing a way forward when appropriate.

Gentlemen, women do not want you to give them a solution however much you feel the need to offer one. Just give them space, a few minutes to recover themselves if they're upset or angry and then move the conversation on. You do not

## *'Gentlemen, women do not want you to give them a solution'*

need to comfort them physically, just give them space and they'll recover themselves more quickly. Sometimes a hug can make people even more upset so an objective and supportive approach is appropriate, from a suitable distance. While working in a male dominated environment, a line manager said to a female staff member, on more than one occasion "I can see that's upset you". She replied, "it hasn't upset me, it's made me really angry", and so the conversation went on. Would he have used the word 'upset' with a male colleague? It seems unlikely. Be mindful of the language you use around your team. Are there elements of it that are gender-biased which are now outdated?

For a woman line managing a male staff member, it can be more difficult to build a conversation, particularly when a perceived criticism has been raised as the staff member's immediate response will probably be to move away from the difficult conversation. In those situations, it can be useful to have a brief, initial conversation about what the problem is and then confirm that a further meeting has been scheduled for the following day, for instance, in order to focus on what happened and how the situation can be improved for the future. That gives the male staff member time to process the initial, perceived criticism and return with a more proactive response the following day. You know your staff and so will be able to judge these situations depending on the individual but thinking about your approach before you enter into a more difficult conversation is useful.

Women are said to have approximately 20,000 words to speak each day (on average) whereas men have approximately

7,000 words[86] so it's easy to see why men and women become frustrated with each other!  Be mindful, if you're managing someone of the opposite gender that they may not share your love or loathing of long conversations so adjust your approach appropriately.  Combining gender with personality type can give a sense of a person's preference for longer conversations.  An introverted woman might talk more than an introverted man and an extroverted man might not talk as much as an extroverted woman.  As you get to know your team members well, their body language will often indicate their preferences although your usual expectations might not be met if you try to talk to them in the middle of a highly complex piece of work, for instance.

Keeping an open mind is crucial when dealing with any aspect of line management.  While you may well know the behaviour you'll expect to see from each person, you can never

## '*Keeping an open mind is crucial when dealing with any aspect of line management.*'

know the full picture of what's happening for every staff member all of the time and so flexibility of approach is important. The great thing about line management and dealing with people generally is that you're constantly learning and the more you learn the more you can apply your experiences to a range of situations.  That allows you to grow in confidence as a line manager and apply a range of techniques more easily, so as your experience increases, your line management practice won't feel as exhausting as it did when you first started out.

## Age

Managing teams with staff members of different ages can be highly productive or it can be hugely challenging, depending on the working relationships between them.  Your team members will take their lead from you, generally so if you're seen to value the diversity of ages, skills and experience then they will too and talking about the strengths of each team member in a meeting has a great value.  Historically, we've seen teams of younger people being managed by an older line manager but those dynamics are changing and a younger line manager can often find themselves managing a team with people who might be significantly older than they are. Does this need to cause problems? Not if both parties are respectful of each other[87]. Staff members might be disrespectful about a line manager who is younger than they are, questioning how they can perform the role when they have less experience. People can forget very quickly that they've not been ambitious, for instance and have been happy to stay in the same role for several years. They might feel threatened when a younger person joins the team and takes on a line management role, even if they don't want that role themselves. A disrespectful response is often about the individual, more than the line manager but that doesn't make it any easier to manage.[88]

It can be tempting to try and befriend your staff members in order to build your working relationships with them but that might not help their perception of you, as they may see that approach as a weaker one. People can be difficult to manage as they're all totally different from one another but if you, as a younger line manager feel that a staff member's approach towards you is disrespectful, it's important to address that behaviour very quickly. This could be the most difficult conversation

> *'if you, as a younger line manager feel that a staff member's approach towards you is disrespectful, it's important to address that behaviour very quickly.'*

you have with a staff member but it's important to show that such behaviour is unacceptable, that you do have the confidence to address it and that you're not prepared for such behaviour to go unchallenged. People will think what they want to ultimately but by showing your professionalism in dealing with a difficult situation assertively, you're showing your authority, skills and confidence as a line manager.

You might say "I believe you have questioned my ability to undertake this role as I'm a younger person". Do not feel that you need to justify yourself in terms of your skills and experience, you have been recruited into the role and so the people who interviewed you have decided that you do have the right skills and experience, you don't have to explain your work history and qualifications to the staff member. The issue is with their unacceptable behaviour, which you deem to be disrespectful and it's important to explain that to them. You might say "is there anything else you would like to talk about, in terms of the dynamics of the team?" and hopefully the staff member will have been shamed into silence by that point, quite rightly. Being disrespectful towards a line manager, whatever their age can be interpreted as bullying and it's useful to make a record of your conversation and advise your own line manager that the conversation has taken place, in case further incidents occur.

Older staff members may be inclined to talk to younger staff members as if they were their own children and again, it's important to address that behaviour very quickly in a one-to-one conversation. Older people can be guilty of thinking that younger people have less to offer but that's not the case. Younger people can have more energy and a willingness to learn which balances out the skills and experience of an older person. All of those skills are valid and a bit like learner drivers, we all had to learn at some point and so kindness and compassion can be demonstrated by sharing skills with colleagues. Older people can be more reluctant to learn new skills whereas a younger person might embrace that challenge more readily. Our skills are different and with a supportive and trusting environment we can complement each other to build an effective team.

A difficult conversation, for a younger line manager with an older member of staff, or vice versa can be a challenge and

> *'A difficult conversation, for a younger line manager with an older member of staff, ... can be a challenge ... the age difference should be put aside'*

whenever possible, the age difference should be put aside in your mind. This is a staff member, a colleague or a line manager and so respect of each other is appropriate, regardless of age. How would you treat someone of a similar age to you? There's no reason why a conversation with a staff member much older or younger than you should be any different to those you'll have with staff members of a similar age. The barriers are only there if you put them there. If you hear comments or conversations relating to age, particularly if there is a derogatory element to them, that must be challenged very quickly. Generalisations are by nature wrong and so generalisations and stereotypes around younger, older or middle-aged people should be challenged. Sometimes there's not a malicious intent but be mindful about office banter which excludes particular groups or focuses on a perceived weaknesses of a particular age group.

**Reasonable Adjustments**
Reasonable adjustments are just that, they're reasonable and while we may expect to make adjustments for a particular gender or age group, that might not always be the case and so a consistent and equitable approach is important. An older staff member might be expected to be more likely to ask for flexibility to accommodate caring responsibilities for a parent but a younger staff member might make that same request. A younger person might be expected to be more likely to make a request for flexibility to accommodate their parental responsibilities. Similarly, an older staff member may make a request to give time to care for their grandchildren. A consistent approach, taken in accordance with your organisational policies is key to maintaining staff engagement. If staff members have a request for support turned down, they're more likely to be accepting of that decision if they can see their treatment has been in line with policy and the treatment of their colleagues. While it can be disappointing to have a request for support or flexibility turned down, there

*'There is a balance to be sought between consistency and line management discretion'*

might be other options available to the staff member and a willingness to consider those maintains staff engagement.

Line management discretion and reasonable adjustments allow a line manager to offer support and flexibility to staff members that allows them to continue to work effectively. If possible, a win-win scenario is the best outcome. However, your discretion and reasonable adjustments are specific to a staff member and don't mean that the support and flexibility that's been made available to one staff member automatically becomes available to everyone else in the team. There is a balance to be sought between consistency and line management discretion which may need to be discussed with your own line manager at some point to agree a wider, organisational response. Re-iterate to other staff members that flexibility and support have been made available to one staff member for a specific reason and possibly for a specific timescale. If they wish to make a similar request, they can do so and that will be considered independently, on its own merits. Most organisational policies will define a right to ask for flexibility, support or reasonable adjustments, not a right for those things to be granted automatically.

After reading this chapter, think about the demographics of your team in terms of age and gender. Is there a good mix and an appreciation of different skills and abilities or does language creep in which could be considered as disrespectful? As with personality types, you can think about the strengths of the team in terms of its demographics, without talking specifically about individuals. Questions such as "what strengths can a younger (and older) person bring to the team?" and "how do men and women work differently?" can develop into an interesting conversation which helps the team get to know each other. In leading the conversation, you might say "this needs to be a respectful conversation which values the differences of everyone here". Humour can be useful sometimes when you're discuss-

## 'Humour can be useful...'

ing the differences between people but be very quick to call out any comments which hint towards criticism, particularly if that seems to be directed at a specific individual. We all have strengths and we all have things we're not so good at. While it can be easy to think 'I wish everyone was like me', there is great value in diversity and an effective discussion can help staff members to recognise and value the strengths, experience and skills of their colleagues.

# Chapter 12

## Performance Management

Performance management takes time[89] and so it can be easier not to bother with it or to meet the organisation's requirements to a bare minimum. That approach can be fine when everything's fine, when your staff are working effectively and workload is going to plan. However, that optimal situation doesn't usually last for long for a variety of reasons and without a performance plan staff cannot be held to account; a line manager has no way to differentiate the performance of their staff without one. High performers are not recognised and rewarded, and under-performers are not challenged which can irritate the high performers who become dis-engaged and at worst, leave the organisation. Workforce wellbeing, organisational strength and resilience are built on honest conversations with staff and performance plans are a key part of that conversation.

Standards and styles of performance management vary greatly across organisations, from those who still use paper-based appraisal systems to those who have embraced technology-based solutions. There can be positives and negatives to all approaches but a good system or process will facilitate a conversation between a line manager and their staff member, show reflections on the previous year from both of you, define the goals, objectives and expectations of the coming year and allow for progress to be monitored regularly, quarterly for instance. The process should also include a training and development section to ensure that even your most experienced staff have the opportunity to do something different sometimes. Job shadowing across your organisation or with customer and supplier organisations can help to build effective working relationships and to develop staff members who are happy to stay in their roles and are not particularly looking to progress. Just because a staff member is not especially ambitious, doesn't mean that you don't need to focus on their development. Development activities are important for maintaining staff engagement and for demonstrating an equitable approach of development to all staff, ambitious or not.

A performance management system or process should not constrain a line manager in having a conversation with their staff member about their performance or behaviour and should not make the process a tick box exercise, which some of the technology-based solutions seem to encourage. Think about how you would like to be treated and try to adapt your systems and processes to match that preference. Would you want to only have one formal conversation about your work performance in a year? It definitely makes the process easier for the line manager but that's not an acceptable level of engagement to ensure wellbeing and effective performance. There will be less-formal conversations in addition to formal reviews of course, via one-to-one meetings but a more formal check in is useful, particularly to ensure the original goals and objectives you agreed are still relevant and appropriate. A lot can happen in 12 months and having a formal review where the staff member's current work responsibilities look nothing like the original goals and objectives is a waste of time for both of you.

A staff member cannot be held to account if their objectives do not reflect their work responsibilities but more importantly you'll be less able to formally recognise and reward that staff member's performance and behaviour if they have completed work which is not defined in their performance plan. They might have performed brilliantly in the last 12 months but those comments will lose impact by being added to the comments section of the performance plan instead of ticking off a number of well-defined objectives, which can then be shown as excellent performance throughout the organisation. Effective performance management systems and processes will enable the accountability of staff for the work they're doing and support a line manager to demonstrate their management of the work responsibilities of their team members.

## Defining Goals and Objectives

The goals and objectives defined as part of a performance management plan need to be achievable. That sounds like an obvious statement, but many have been seen over the years which are not, so it's important to consider whether an objective can be given a 'yes' or 'no' answer in terms of "did you achieve that?". An objective is not a task but individual tasks can be defined as part of the objective itself.

**For example:**

**Objective:** To have improved the reporting process to meet additional client requirements by the end of the financial year.

- Meet with the client to identify their additional reporting requirements by xx/xx/xx.

- Produce three sample reports for the client's review and agree the format of reports for the next financial year by xx/xx/xx.

- Confirm progress regularly at one-to-one meetings with your line manager.

- Produce a report by the end of Q3 to confirm proposed changes to the Management team.

While the example shown is quite general, in practice more specific requirements can be defined to align the objective to the staff member's work responsibilities.

The conversation in reviewing the objective might sound something like this:

**Line Manager (LM)    Staff member (SM)**

**LM:** "On this next objective to revise the client reports, did you achieve that?"

**SM:** "Yes, I did. It didn't go quite to plan but we got there in the end."

**LM:** "So, let's look at the tasks first, did you achieve all of those?"

**SM:** "One of the dates was missed because my contact at the client's office was off sick for a week but other than that I did achieve the dates."

**LM:** "Great stuff, talk me through the process then, what worked well, and what was more difficult?"

And so the conversation progresses but at the very start, the staff member can confirm the objective was achieved because of the way it was defined.  If you have performance management objectives which do not allow that 'yes' or 'no' answer to the question 'did you achieve that?', think about re-wording them ahead of your next review meeting.

Performance management objectives don't need to stay the same for the whole year.  They might do, if the staff member is in a role which generally doesn't change but if their work responsibilities change because they're asked to support a specific project for instance, their performance objectives should be updated, if the project will continue for an extended period.  Line manager comments can be added to a performance plan to indicate the performance objectives have been revised and redefined.  As your confidence in defining objectives builds this process will take less time although it can feel laborious initially.  It can be useful to ask the staff member to try to define their own objectives ahead of a review meeting as they will know the specifics of their work responsibilities and that can save time during your meeting.

Objectives should be agreed, not imposed so it's important to discuss whether the staff member feels their objectives are achievable and to agree a balance of what you both think is feasible for the year or quarter ahead.  They may over-stretch themselves, on completion dates for instance so building in some contingency is important too.  There will always be things that get in the way of progress, so setting a more realistic target date, of a month later than you would both like an objective to be achieved for instance shows that you recognise that progress is not always straight forward and gives the staff member the leeway to achieve against a range of objectives.  If they do deliver against the objective a month ahead of time, they have exceeded your expectations and it's important to allow people to do that.  As objectives are defined, consider how your staff member can meet and exceed the objectives and your expectations.
    Performance grading varies greatly.  One organisation described its staff's performance as 'acceptable' or 'unacceptable' which staff members felt gave no scope for anyone to be great

or amazing if they put the work in. Staff members left their performance reviews feeling that their hard work had not been recognised by the organisation, even though their line managers did recognise the value of their hard work to their clients. The line managers became frustrated, as they felt constrained by the organisational approach to performance reviews and recognised how it dis-engaged their staff.

Make sure your staff can see that levels of performance are differentiated, to show that under-performance and amazing performance will both be recognised. It doesn't always matter what the terminology is, but have more scope than acceptable and unacceptable. That approach gives staff members very little to aspire to and can impact on their level of engagement. With time available, this can be a great exercise for a staff engagement group, to define what they would like the organisation's performance gradings to be.

Be wary of defining objectives which are along the lines of 'carry on doing your job to a good standard'. Objectives should be specific and even the most general of roles can have specific objectives. The following sample objectives may be useful.

- Proactive working – plan and deliver work proactively to meet required deadlines. Identify and escalate issues as appropriate.

When asked "did you achieve that?" a staff member can give a yes or no answer and provide evidence to give specific examples of when they acted proactively. The need for evidence to be collected and details of what that might look like (emails for instance) should be confirmed as the objective is set.

The staff member has the primary responsibility for collating evidence to demonstrate the delivery of their objective but the line manager may also collect supplementary evidence.

- Proactive working – Develop a survey to seek feedback from the teams' clients as to how they perceive our service.

Tasks can be defined to show a breakdown of the steps required to meet this objective.

Tasks may include:

- Work with two other team members to develop a sample survey for review by the team by the end of Q1.

- Identify specific clients to be approached for feedback and confirm their contact details by the second week of Q2.

- Develop an email to be sent ahead of the survey, to introduce it, explain its purpose and the nature of the outcomes.

- Send email and survey on the defined dates.

- Follow up completion and send reminder emails to clients who have not responded one week after the survey close date.

- Collate the survey responses and present the results at the Sept team meeting, to agree next steps.

Objectives

- Team working – work in support of other team members and offer assistance as required.

- Team working – work with two colleagues to issue the client feed back survey and demonstrate the benefits of working together.

- Relationship building – Proactively build effective work relationships with clients and demonstrate the benefits to the team and wider organisation.

- Relationship building – Develop a 10-minute presentation to show the work of the team, to be delivered to four other teams within the organisation.

Tasks may include:

- Develop a presentation to detail the work of the team for sign off with your line manager, by the end of May 20xx.

- Contact four Team Leaders to explain the purpose of the presentation (to build effective work relationships across the organisation) and request time for its delivery in one of their team meetings by the end of Q2.

- Report on progress to the team in our October team meeting and lead a discussion to agree next steps.

- Training and development – work to achieve the requirements of the training and development plan and identify two further development opportunities by the end of Q2.

- Specific projects – Manage the delivery of (the project), reporting progress monthly, identifying and escalating issues as appropriate.

Tasks can be added to each objective to ensure specific requirements have been defined. To exceed an objective a staff member can deliver ahead of schedule, deliver a wider remit than was originally agreed or deliver a quality of work which is over and above your original expectation.

**Training and Development**
Training and development plans are an important part of a performance plan[90]. Whether the staff member is ambitious or not, it's important to factor an element of development into their role each year to ensure their level of engagement doesn't drop. It can be easy to overlook those staff who are great in their roles and are viewed as a safe pair of hands but even the most loyal staff member will start to look around for other roles if they see other staff members undertaking development tasks

*'It can be easy to overlook those staff who are great in their roles and are viewed as a safe pair of hands'*

when they're not. It can send a strong message, regardless of whether it's true or not, that they have become part of the furniture, that they always do a great job so you expect that of them as standard and that you value their contribution less than that of other, more ambitious staff.

The core strength and resilience of your organisation will be built on staff who are:

- Happy in their roles.

- Not looking to move away from the organisation.

- Great at their job.

Their loyalty and great service should be rewarded with engagement and development, not by being overlooked for a more ambitious few.

**Task**
Do you have staff that you view in this way, as a safe pair of hands that can always be relied upon to turn up and do a great job? Be mindful of this as you complete their next performance review.
Make sure aspects of development are factored into all staff performance plans to reduce the risk of losing the most reliable and dedicated among them.
     Training elements of a performance plan focus on more formal training requirements but development can include a range of activities, to include:

- Job shadowing, within the same team to build contingency and across other teams in the organisation and partner organisations, clients and suppliers to build effective work relationships internally and externally.

- Seeking feedback from clients on a range of services.

- Training colleagues to ensure effective levels of cover in case of absence.

- Representing the team at organisational meetings.

- Taking on specific roles such as a staff representative, staff engagement lead or team wellbeing lead.

- Horizon scanning, identifying potential changes in client or supplier requirements.

- Collating information, taking responsibility for collating specific information on behalf of the team and providing regular updates at team meetings.

- Awareness raising - delivering awareness sessions to other teams within the organisation to explain the work of your own team and being a first point of contact for enquiries.

- Being a First Aider or Fire Marshall.

- Delivering welcome sessions for new staff joining the team to 'show them the ropes' and being a first point of contact.

## Challenging Under-Performance Effectively[91]

A performance plan is an effective tool for managing a staff member's performance and behaviour, either for demonstrating great work and achievement, or under-performance. By defining objectives, with specific tasks and timescales, the work required from a staff member is made very clear. On review, their achievement or under-performance can also be clear, which will inform your conversation about next steps. In the case of under-performance, there may well be circumstances beyond the individual's control which have delayed delivery but if they consistently fail to deliver against the defined requirements, the performance plan will provide the evidence to initiate more formal action, should that be required.

Without a performance plan, it can be very difficult to challenge and manage under-performance, especially as part of a formal action so there is a value to ensuring performance plans are up to date for all staff, to give you, their line manager structured evidence as to how well your team is performing. No workplace stands still so your performance plans can reflect that, even for those staff who do not have great variety in their roles. Objectives around proactive work and team-working can always be used to demonstrate an ongoing requirement for the staff member to actively seek opportunities to support their colleagues, for instance and to offer evidence as to how that was undertaken. How that looks this year is very unlikely to look the same in 12 months time, as the workplace around you will change even if the staff member's role doesn't and so further evidence can be collected.

To support discussions around apparent under-performance, the performance plan can offer an effective structure to that conversation. You will have your own preference of how the conversation is managed but make sure the staff member is given an opportunity to explain why delivery has not occurred as expected, either individually as objectives and tasks are reviewed or collectively at the start of the review. There might be issues that you weren't aware of which have hindered progress and require your intervention to allow work to move forward. If that is the case, it's useful to discuss how issues could've been escalated sooner, if that's appropriate.

With the performance plan as a structure, it can become clear very quickly whether a staff member is struggling to achieve their objectives for genuine reasons, which might require your intervention, or if they're not motivated to deliver against the objectives that were agreed. If a lack of motivation is apparent, it's appropriate to ask why that is to try and understand if additional support is required. A situation might exist, either in work or outside of it, which is affecting the staff member's ability to deliver against their defined objectives. Very few people are looking to under-perform consistently; we spend a lot of time at work and most staff will want to be there, to some degree and perform their duties well. Our work lives are much more rewarding if we do a good job and so if a staff member is under-performing it's worth taking some time to understand why that is.

A staff member may say that they feel overwhelmed by the objectives since they were set and don't now think they're achievable, particularly if a more structured approach is new to them. It might be appropriate to relax deadlines slightly or reduce the number of tasks attributed to each objective. The number of tasks might stay the same but the staff member might feel more assured if they're only added one quarter at a

time.  Some people like to see a full list to know what they have
to do to achieve something, whereas others can feel daunted by
it, so a flexible approach from you can secure their continued
engagement.

When challenging under-performance, it's important
to give a staff member an opportunity to improve so you may
want to revise deadlines or the tasks to be completed.  Depending on the objective and the work to be completed, don't leave
a further review until the next quarter's meeting.  If you ex-
tend deadlines by a month, schedule a review meeting for one
month's time and discuss progress in one-to-one meetings in
the meantime.  Demonstrating the active management of the
work required from your staff member can have two effects; as
an assertive approach is being taken to under-performance, the
staff member will either respond well and improve their work
delivery or they may well seek other options for employment.
Either way, the performance plan has enabled you to assess
the staff member's performance, address any issues and review
their response to under-performance, which can inform your
decision-making on next steps.  Without a performance plan,
that process is much more difficult to manage.

After reading this chapter, think about the performance
review systems and processes that are available to you.  Are
they effective?  Do they support an ongoing conversation with
each staff member and the monitoring of progress in relation to

> *'...think about the performance*
> *review systems and processes*
> *that are available to you.*
> *Are they effective?'*

performance and behaviour?  Is your own performance review,
completed by your line manager effective?  If not, it might be
time to apply your learning to your own performance review and
show your line manager how it's done!  As the person being
reviewed it's appropriate to propose objectives and add a narra-
tive regarding progress ahead of the review meeting.  Your line
manager will probably be delighted if you do so and that can be
a great way to demonstrate a more proactive approach.  Performance reviews allow you to hold under-performers to account,

to offer support and assistance with areas for development but they also give you the opportunity to shine. If you're delivering effective line management, which supports the strength and resilience of your team and the wider organisation, you should definitely make sure that's documented on your review!

If you feel that your existing performance management processes are a tick box exercise then you can almost guarantee that your staff will feel the same way. They will know that they're not being recognised formally for their great work or challenged on areas where they need to improve which is almost certainly affecting the level of engagement, commitment and loyalty from your staff. Performance management can feel like a chore but delivered effectively, it allows you to define expectations of performance and behaviour, monitor performance, recognise great work and define and support areas for improvement. That process gives great strength and resilience to the management of your workforce.

# Chapter 13

## Strength and Resilience

Resilience is important[92].  Whilst it's good to think about and anticipate difficulties in both the personal and professional aspects of life, it's impossible to predict exactly what the future will bring.  In managing stress and anxiety, it's important to remember that only your response to events can be controlled; often you'll have very little control over day-to-day events and the reactions of other people.  By controlling your response to an event or situation, you can control the outcome of it[93], although that can take time, practice and reflection to recognise.  Personal, team and organisational resilience allow us to stay strong, to react proactively when difficult events occur and not

*'Personal, team and organisational resilience allow us to stay strong, to react proactively when difficult events occur and not feel beaten by them.'*

feel beaten by them.  It can be difficult if you hit a run of negative events and that's when your strength, determination, tenacity and resilience can be tested.  In this chapter we focus on the three specific aspects of strength and resilience.

### Personal Resilience

Psychological resilience is defined as an individual's ability to successfully cope with adversity and to be able to bounce back from a negative experience with 'competent functioning'[94].  Most people have a level of resilience but it also can be learned and developed to give them greater strength in dealing with negative events.  Resilient individuals develop healthy coping mechanisms which allow them to effectively navigate their way

*'Resilient individuals develop healthy coping mechanisms...'*

through difficulties and crises with more optimistic attitudes and positive emotions.  That doesn't mean that a more resilient

© 2019 Karen Warren

person can deal with anything that's thrown at them, they have levels of tolerance just like everyone else but a more resilient person will generally have a more positive cycle of thinking which does allow them to bounce back more quickly when difficult events occur[95].

As with stress, our levels of resilience can be impacted by a range of factors, to include physical and mental health difficulties, financial pressures, ongoing stressful situations and relationship problems.  Someone who is usually perceived to be a very resilient person can demonstrate out of character behaviours when other factors are at play in their lives.  It can be tempting to assume that a usually resilient person is always OK but that's not the case.  Everyone needs a level of support; however resilient and independent they're perceived to be and as a line manager it's important that assumptions are not made which lead to inconsistent levels of support being offered to your team members.  Just because someone looks fine, it doesn't always mean that they are.  The immediate effects of stress can be hidden [96].

Personal resilience is supported by good wellbeing [97] -

•      By eating healthily.

•      Exercising.

•      Taking time out for yourself.

•      Identifying options for support.

By focusing on these aspects of wellbeing, you will be embedding healthy resilience into your life.

Good personal resilience can be developed in a behavioural sense -

•      by allowing yourself to make mistakes sometimes.

•      not giving yourself a hard time if you do make mistakes.

- allowing yourself to learn.

We allow children to make mistakes and learn from them but as adults we take a much harder stance and can become self-critical if mistakes are made [98].

Line management is a good example of a role that can only be taught to some extent, as the staff you manage will always be unique individuals and so what works with one, may not work well with another. By adapting the general guidelines of line management, you can work effectively with a range of staff and find ways to build effective relationships with them. A 'one size fits all' approach will not support effective line management and may well have a detrimental effect on your relationships with your team. It may feel like a consistent way of managing people and in a way, it is that but treating people as if they're all the same won't get the best out of them. The consistent application of organisational policies can be achieved alongside treating people as individuals.

Line management and maintaining your personal resilience can be about trusting your instincts. Once you know your team well, you'll be able to see if someone is acting out of character and can arrange to talk to them about it. By supporting staff members effectively in this way and offering support in a timely manner, you can support your own resilience in the knowledge that you're working effectively to identify potential issues and take appropriate action. There will always be issues to surprise you, as some people can keep their difficulties hidden but if you're having regular one-to-one meetings with each staff member and develop trusting relationships with them, you can sleep more soundly in the knowledge that issues are less likely to surprise you.

The process of line management allows you to learn constantly as you learn about the different styles of your staff

## *'The process of line management allows you to learn constantly...'*

members and what motivates them. If you think you know it all already, you've become less open-minded about what can be presented to you in terms of a staffing issue and it's worth reflecting on that. If you've worked with the same team of people for a long time you might all have become very used to each other's ways and there may be a value to doing something different as a team event, for instance to re-energise your relationships. It's unlikely that you know everything about all of your team, even if you think you do, so by asking staff members to tell the rest of the team something that they don't already know about them, you can gain a new perspective on each person.

Asking for help is a sign of strength [99] so if you're struggling, either with your own resilience or in the line management of a staff member, it's worth asking a trusted colleague, possibly your own line manager or a member of the HR team, if you have one, for their advice. Be mindful of confidentiality whenever you seek support, especially if you work in a smaller organisation where an individual can be easily identified during a conversation. It's acceptable to seek advice and support from an external source but again, be very mindful of confidentiality of the staff member if you're seeking line management advice.

**A Good Energy Day**
A useful task, either as a personal exercise or a team one, is to focus on what a good energy day looks like for you. So often you can make your way through work days dealing with issues, attending meetings and resolving issues but if you don't consciously connect with what makes it a good day, you might struggle to tap into those positive energy days even when they happen.

What is a good energy day for you?

• At work?

• At home?

• With family and friends?

• On your own?

Make sure you factor some of the elements of a good energy day into your week, to give a balance of the more demanding aspects of your role and the ones you really enjoy. That supports

good resilience.  If you enjoy one-to-one conversations with staff members, schedule
appointments each week to give a balance of your work responsibilities.  If you like one-to-one meetings less but enjoy delivering presentations for instance, try to factor that aspect of work into your week or month as much as possible.  Everyone needs a balance; if you're not a huge fan of completing performance reviews but leave them all until the week before the completion deadline that'll give you a very difficult week and your resilience is likely to be affected.  If the meetings are booked intermittently across the four or five weeks ahead of the completion deadline, they're less likely to feel like such an onerous task.  That helps your resilience.

Is it running you or are you running it?  You can ask yourself that question to make yourself think more consciously about what you're doing, to question and recognise the value you're adding to a situation or piece of work and to consider the impact your work is having on your physical, emotional and mental health.  If 'it' (your work) is running you, you may well be less effective and reacting to work issues as opposed to managing them proactively.

There will always be an element of reactivity to anyone's work but if you're running 'it', you're making more constructive decisions, which support your wellbeing and resilience.  Your personal resilience can diminish if you're only reacting to other people's needs and not doing the things that you want to do. Line management can easily become about everyone else and not you, so it's important to keep a focus on your own health, wellbeing and resilience as well as supporting the needs of your team.

**Team Resilience**

Team resilience can have a very operational focus in the first instance.  Can your staff members cover each other's roles during holiday and sickness absence?  Do your work systems allow for another staff member to pick up the work of a colleague if a customer calls in with a query?  Can you work from home, knowing the team will continue to work effectively in your absence?  Do staff complete handover notes when they're due to take planned leave to ensure their work can be progressed appropriately in their absence?  Can all staff see your and their colleagues' calendars to know where they are and when they're likely to return, in the event of a query from a customer? Are staff expected to respond to queries on behalf of their colleagues? The answers to these questions will relate to the type of work that you do and so some might not be applicable but it's important that there are clear expectations that staff will cover each other's roles and respond to queries on behalf of a colleague in nearly all teams. That approach builds the strength and resilience of the team.

Team resilience can also be developed by giving staff members the time and space to get to know each other well and to recognise and value the strengths of their colleagues[100]. Not all teams will get on with each other and not all teams will want to socialise together but all staff members have strengths and by giving time to team activities, those strengths can be identified. One approach is to use some of the questions detailed below in a team meeting.

**Team activity** - Build a dialogue with your team

- What do you think we do well as a team?

- What do we do less well?

- What does a good day look like for you, in work and out side work?

- What do you enjoy about your job?

- What do you enjoy less about your job?

- Tell us something we don't know about you.

- Who's in your life that makes you smile?

- If we had a £1,000 to spend, what would your choice of team away day be?

- Who inspires you?

- Would you come in tomorrow if you won the lottery tonight?

By demonstrating role model behaviours, a line manager can encourage staff members to offer positive feedback when they see someone deal with something well. Sometimes we struggle to find the right language to recognise and reward other people, but a simple 'you're good at that', 'I like how you do that', 'that's a great job!' or even a 'that's flippin brilliant!' can make someone feel valued and that their hard work has been recognised. You don't need to be a line manager to offer someone praise; that can be done peer-to-peer as well. As long as the tone of the feedback is respectful and sincere, it's difficult to go wrong.

By asking the team what they think you do well as a team, you're supporting their personal and team resilience. A psychologically safe team will feel comfortable to acknowledge

## '*A psychologically safe team will feel comfortable to acknowledge any mistakes...*'

any mistakes as they'll know that their colleagues will offer support to put a situation right or identify ways to improve. Effective teams work well together but they also generate ideas for change, which will support the strength and resilience of the team as well as the wider organisation.

### Organisational Resilience

Organisational resilience can also have an operational focus in the first instance, as contingency planning is an important part of ensuring the continued delivery of products and services[101]. 'What if' questions can help an organisation to plan for unexpected events, to consider the impact of a need to relocate for instance or to deal with a major incident at your workplace. The evaluation of risk is calculated on scales of impact and likelihood, and sometimes the big questions can be useful to start the development of contingency plans.

For example:

- What if a plane crash landed on our workplace premises overnight?

- What if all electrical and Wi-Fi services were unavailable for a week or a month?

- What if all our staff got food poisoning at one time?

- What if the whole area was flooded for a week?

- What if our premises were requisitioned by the military to support a major incident response for a month?

- What if 75% of our staff, who are in a lottery syndicate win?

While the likelihood is low for all of these situations, the impact would be high and so contingency plans will need to be adopted. Do you have plans?

- Would your staff know what to do in the event of an emergency overnight at your workplace?

- Do you have an agreed method of contact in the event of a major event?

Depending on the size of your workplace and the nature of your work, your contingency plans might be small or elaborate. As a minimum, it's important to have a conversation with your workforce to ensure they're aware of the action to be taken in the event of an unexpected situation, which may require them to call a central number to access information updates, for instance.

Organisational resilience can also take the form of training and job shadowing across the organisation, to build effective relationships between teams, build awareness of the responsibilities and challenges facing each team and to offer wider contingency to cover staff absence. Working effectively across departments can help to develop a positive team working culture where staff understand the need for flexibility and embrace opportunities for variety by working with other colleagues.  This approach can be led by example as staff see their Managers work well together and support each other when difficulties arise.  Organisational strength and resilience are developed from a proactive, open-minded and adaptable approach to work issues and by demonstrating these approaches, staff will be encouraged to demonstrate the same behaviours themselves.

After reading this chapter, think about your personal resilience in the first instance and that of your team.  Are there

## '...think about your personal resilience in the first instance and that of your team'

aspects of development on your training and development plan that support your role as a line manager and allow you to take time away from the team for your own personal development? Line management is challenging and can feel tiring and relentless, as staff members can forget that you have your own work responsibilities and other things going on, outside of work which might affect your own performance and behaviour.  If you don't have specific training and development opportunities that support your own development it's very much worth contacting your training providers to see what training they offer, or finding out what's available in your local area.  Find out what training opportunities your customers and suppliers access too, as training with partner organisations can be a great way to build effective relationships and sometimes reduce costs.

Does your team have opportunities to take time out for a team meeting once a month or are you too busy to do that? The cycle of short-term perspective and reactive responses discussed in chapter 1 is an easy cycle of performance and behaviour to get into and one which doesn't allow time for team meetings, one-to-ones, training and development or performance reviews.  If you feel that there's not time to do any of those things, that could be an indication that your culture of wellbeing needs to change, to ensure your workforce is well and your

© 2019 Karen Warren

organisation has great strength and resilience.

*'Line management is challenging and can feel tiring and relentless, as staff members can forget that you have your own work responsibilities and other things going on, outside of work which might affect your own performance and behaviour.'*

# Chapter 14

## Your Leadership Legacy

We all have a choice of what our legacy will be; in life, in work and in our relationships. It sounds a bit morbid but if your sudden demise was announced on the ten o'clock news tonight, would the people you work with now and have worked with in the past rush to attend your funeral or pay their respects? To tell your family and loved ones about the support you gave them while you worked together? You can't all be best friends and not everyone will like your style, for a range of reasons but if your approach is supportive and consistent people will usually respect your working practices, even if you're very different people.

## Your Values and Beliefs

Your values and beliefs are very personal so they will not always be shared by the people you work with. If honesty is a strong value for you and a staff member is not reflecting progress on a piece of work accurately, that will feel frustrating for you but it's important that you don't over-react because that's such a strong value for you. Honesty is important of course, as

### *'Honesty is important...'*

is accurately reporting progress on pieces of work but not everyone will feel as strongly about that as you might. It's just different. By demonstrating the impact of the issue, along with the subsequent problems the lack of accurate reporting has caused you or colleagues, you can demonstrate why honesty and accurate reporting are so important. It can be very easy to think that everyone feels as we do with our personal values but that's not the case.

As you get to know your team you will identify staff members' values, you will see what's important to them and the strengths that gives you as a team. As with gender and age, it can be very easy to work more closely with those team members who share similar values to you but be wary of excluding others. As long as the work is done in a timely manner, to an acceptable standard, a level of flexibility in how it gets done can increase staff engagement. If your preference and value is to always to aim to deliver a piece of work days ahead of a deadline and you have a staff member who has a more last-minute approach to things but who always delivers, albeit at the last minute, who's right and who's wrong?

As long as the work gets delivered on time and to an acceptable standard, you, as a line manager might have to tolerate the fact that others deliver in a different way to you. As the line manager, your way is not necessarily the right way, you should not dictate the 'how' of the work to be completed, generally, but just 'what' needs to be done. Be very mindful not to micro-manage staff members or take a hero leadership approach, as it's very likely to dis-engage people.

> ### 'Be very mindful not to micro-manage staff members or take a hero leadership approach...'

It can be easy to view people with different values as lower performers than they actually are, just because their style of delivery doesn't align to your preferences. Be wary of the statement "if it were me...." in the context of how work should be completed. A different style might not make you feel comfortable but if you dictate the 'how' staff members may well dis-engage from you over time and look to move on. They're adults, not children and being given the freedom to work to their own values, beliefs and preferences can help them flourish in their roles and become highly effective and highly engaged staff members. That makes you a great leader and together you can effectively support the strength and resilience of your team and organisation.

Personal values can be a good topic for a team meeting, or part of it, to encourage staff members to identify their top three values, the things that are really important to them and to discuss the differences with their colleagues. Sometimes understanding people's values can help us to understand their

> ### 'Sometimes understanding people's values can help us to understand their behaviour'

behaviour, especially when those values are influenced by life events which they often are. By giving the team time to think and talk about the things that are important to them, you can help them to build more effective working relationships which are underpinned by a more specific understanding of what motivates each person and why that motivation exists.

## Demonstrating Role Model Behaviours

As frustrating as it can be, a line manager doesn't always get to 'let their hair down' with staff and 'be one of the guys'. If you let your guard down and behave in a way that you would usually deem unacceptable it can be almost guaranteed that at least one staff member will observe that incident and squirrel it away for a later time. Staff members observe their line managers and their management teams; they're watching to see how individuals behave and react in particular situations. They might observe how a line manager deals with a stressful situation or a personal disappointment. They'll observe how an under-performing staff member is dealt with and align that treatment to their own personal values, which may or may not be useful. People will always have an opinion so while you, as a line manager are human and can 'let your hair down' with your team to some extent, remember that you might need to have a difficult conversation with one of those staff members in the future and so they still need to respect the behaviours that you demonstrate. There's not one rule for you and one rule for them as your team. Your staff will expect you to demonstrate the performance and behaviours that you expect of them and if

> *'Your staff will expect you to demonstrate the performance and behaviours that you expect of them...'*

they see that from you it'll be much easier to hold them to account if they under-perform or behave poorly.

Everyone can have a bad day and saying that can be a good way of explaining why the team might not see your usual performance and behaviours. Honesty if you're struggling shows an appreciation and understanding of people working through difficult times. Your honesty is likely to encourage honesty from your staff members if they're struggling and that can help you identify potential problems sooner than if staff members are reluctant to indicate a problem because they never see that from you. Your team meetings don't need to turn into group therapy sessions but by saying something like "I'm having a difficult week this week; my customers aren't returning my calls and I've got three reports to complete by Friday", you can let staff members see that you can struggle, just as they can. It's not about seeking sympathy from your team but very factually explaining why things are difficult. Be mindful of getting into a competition to see who's struggling the most though, especially as a line manager. Staff will have less sympathy for you generally because you're probably paid more than they are so find the right balance between "phew, I'm struggling" and "poor me".

**Task**
Think about your behaviours in the workplace. Would you define them as role model behaviours? Do you perform and behave in the ways that you expect your staff members to?

Being friends with certain staff members can create difficulties, especially if the staff you're less friendly with perceive that more favourable treatment is offered to others. Consistency is important, regardless of personal relationships. Staff can be aware of friendships between their line manager and other team members, it just needs to be managed carefully. The line manager's authority should be equal across the team, not patchy and dependent on who your pals are. Staff members will very quickly dis-engage from you if they perceive favouritism towards their colleagues.

Sometimes a line manager can try too hard to be friends with their team and that can backfire, particularly if they try to build those relationships by being critical of others in the organisation. While a staff member may well appear to agree with the criticism at the time, they're likely to store that incident away as unprofessional behaviour and voice their opinions on it to others, which could affect your reputation across the team and wider organisation. If you have criticisms of other people in the organisation be very careful about who you express them to, as relationships and allegiances can change over time and people can have very long memories.

## Engagement and Communication

When was the last time you spent time with your team with no planned, work-related agenda, either in work or socially? Did you have a Christmas party but spend much of it talking about work? Work is what bonds us as colleagues and so often social events particularly can be a great way of trying to build more effective relationships but if we don't find out anything new about the people there, is that the most productive use of everyone's time? Social events for work colleagues have a value of course but finding out what suits the whole team can be challenging. A pub, bar or restaurant environment may well suit more extroverted staff members but alienate the more introverted ones and quieter, more reflective pursuits might not be favoured by the more extroverted staff members. It's very hard to please all of the people, all of the time so the key to success can be found in engagement and consultation.

People will usually show a level of flexibility if they feel

*'People will usually show a level of flexibility...'*

their preferences are considered at some point so it might be agreed that a team night out will be held in a restaurant one month and then be offered as a country walk the following month. Flexibility is key so let the team negotiate a balance that they find comfortable. As the line manager, you will need to facilitate those negotiations and if quieter staff members are being over-ridden then you can help them find their voice. An anonymous ballot can be useful with a number of options proposed as sometimes a more extroverted staff member will enjoy the peace and quiet of a country walk and a more introverted staff member will happily embrace the noise and chatter of a local restaurant. Engaging with your staff members and facilitating their discussions shows that you have an open approach

*'Engaging with your staff members and facilitating their discussions shows that you have an open approach'*

© 2019 Karen Warren

to decision-making and will make an effort to ensure every team member voices their opinion.

Communication between staff and managers can sometimes be one-way, often because time pressures give little time for much else but a lack of two-way communication can impact on staff engagement and organisational strength and resilience. If staff members are interested and engaged in their work, they will often have ideas for change, which can range from small tweaks to processes which make everyday life easier for a few people, to major changes which might ultimately win the organisation new contracts or access to additional funding for instance. The answers are often on the 'shop floor', with the people who deliver your front-line services[102]. If you don't find a

## *'The answers are often ...with the people who deliver your front-line services...'*

way to engage and communicate with those staff members, rich sources of ideas for change and development might well be lost.

From a simple suggestion box to a more strategic innovation competition, methods of two-way communication can be developed to ensure ideas and suggestions for change are sought from staff members to show their thoughts and contributions are valued. Find a way to tell your wider workforce about the ideas that have been put forward. No idea is too small, even if a staff member does feel self-conscious about other people finding out about their suggestion. If an idea can save money, make money or make working practices and communication easier, then it has a value to the organisation.

Team meetings are a great forum for two-way communication and a meeting without an agenda can be a wonderful thing. The questions 'what are we doing well?' and 'what can we improve on?' are great for offering an open forum for the thoughts and suggestions of your team. If staff members don't engage in those conversations, that could be an indication of their level of dis-engagement so stick with that approach, even if it's not successful at first. Team meetings can be used to review suggestions and next steps for each one can be managed, in terms of assigning a staff member or a few staff members to work together to identify the costs associated with the proposed change for instance, with an ask that an update is given at the next meeting.  Suggestions can't always be implemented so if that's the case, it's important that an explanation is given as to why that is the case.

It might be that further information is required and the staff member who made the suggestion is tasked to complete more research in order for an informed decision to be made but all suggestions must be seen to be considered, even if they seem outlandish at first.  Some of the greatest innovations have come from suggestions that sounded that way at first!  Being open to new ideas shows that you value and respect the contributions of your staff members and that will help to build effec-

## 'Being open to new ideas shows that you value and respect the contributions of your staff members...'

tive working relationships, with strength and resilience.

After reading this chapter, think about what the legacy of your line management style will be.  Is it as you would like it to be right now?  If not, think about the changes you'll make and if you need support from your own line manager to make those things happen.  Is there more training you'd like to access? If so, find the course, confirm the cost and consider the logistics of you attending.  Email the request to your line manager, propose the date that you'd like to attend and confirm that you will add the details to your training and development plan.  If you take a less assertive approach to accessing training and in effect add 'line management (or other) training for ****' to your line manager's to do list, it's unlikely you'll attend that course in the next 12 months.

If you offer the solution and confirm that logistically it's viable for you to attend, it's much more likely to happen as you would prefer.  You have to make things easy for people to say yes!

If your legacy is not where you would like it to be, that doesn't mean it can't change.  Behaviours can change and so the legacy of your line management can too.  It might be that you need some help with your confidence for instance, to help

© 2019 Karen Warren  **187**

you communicate more assertively and you can look to access learning materials in work or away from work to help you to do that. Aspiring to be a great line manager and to leave a great legacy is a great ambition but it doesn't mean that you can flick a switch to be that person tomorrow. Every staff member is different so there will always be challenges. You'll never stop learning as a line manager!

# Chapter 15

## Is Your Workforce Well?

This book has considered several aspects of workforce wellbeing,
including:

- why workforce wellbeing is important.

- how to develop an effective culture of wellbeing.

- how to identify a problem.

- how to manage difficult conversations.

The first step is to know whether your workforce is well[103] and as an employer or line manager you should know if that's the case.

Wellbeing is about physical, mental and emotional health, and the individual's ability to undertake the role they're paid to do. While it's possible to empathise with someone in a difficult situation, you're not a charity and so very honest, kind and compassionate conversations are a necessity to ensure your team and your organisation can function as effectively as possible.

So often in business we focus on finance and budgets, the delivery of products and services, sales and marketing, finding new customers and product and service development. Those aspects of business are very important but if there's little or no investment in the people who deliver each aspect of that business, your organisational strength and resilience will not be

*'...if there's little or no investment in the people who deliver each aspect of that business, your organisational strength and resilience will not be developed or sustained.'*

© 2019 Karen Warren

developed or sustained. The risk of failure in your business is increasing right in front of you. Your workforce is at the core of your organisation; treated well they will perform and behave effectively. Treated less well they might be present but functioning much less effectively. Potentially, additional staff will be recruited to fill the gaps but they will absorb the culture of your organisation over time and so might also become less effective.

Many employers have watched high performing staff walk away from their organisation and have endeavoured to replace that person's skills. But staff members are not just 'bottoms (U.S.A. = 'butts') on seats' they're an amazing collection of skills, experience and a willingness to support their team and organisation to succeed, so finding a replacement with the exact same skills, experience and talent can be very challenging. High performing staff will often move on, that's a fact but if they leave knowing that they've been supported to develop and progress by their line manager and the wider organisation, they'll leave with great wellbeing. That wellbeing will raise your reputation with the staff member's new organisation as they're likely to talk positively of their past experiences and in the longer term, they're more likely to come back to you for a more senior position. Win-win. The staff member is also likely to use your line management style as a template for their own style and that's a great way for your legacy and investment in that individual to live on, and that can be an amazing feeling. If a staff member leaves your organisation with a lesser sense of wellbeing for whatever reason, your personal and organisational reputation are more likely to be tarnished as difficult experiences are relayed to others.

## Facilitating Conversations

As discussed in chapter 5, it's important to be able to facilitate a conversation with a staff member once a problem has been identified but in a wider cultural sense it's important that conversations with your workforce become the norm; to celebrate successes, to work through change and more difficult times and to update staff on what's changing. If staff feel they're being kept in the dark they'll make up their own stories, based on small nuggets of information they glean from a range of sources. If you want your workforce to hear one message about your culture, strategic and operational changes, and your plans for great workforce wellbeing you need to find a way of giving out one message. In smaller organisations it can be easier to bring staff members together in one place, to hear one person speak and give staff the opportunity to ask questions. Don't feel frustrated by being asked questions; staff who ask questions are engaged and interested in your organisation! Not having any questions asked is more of a signal for concern.

In larger organisations, facilitating a conversation with the whole workforce can be more challenging, so asking them how they would like to receive information updates can be useful. You'll never please all of the people all of the time on this one as our preferences for communication can differ greatly but the power of a video update might be a great way to give the same update to every staff member, with follow up discussions held in team meetings. That way every staff member has a consistent message, not something that's lost in translation as it's passed around the organisation. Newsletters and blogs have their place for information updates but a four- or five-minute video can contain a huge amount of information and staff are more likely to engage with that format than having to read pages of information. We live in a digital age and you can make that work for you.

As an employer or manager, your role is to communicate with your teams, to relay information and direction, and to receive information back. If staff members become accustomed to having two-way conversations about the performance, culture, changes to the team and the wider organisation, they're more likely to offer comments and suggestions proactively, without a prompt or meeting with you as they recognise that as part of your organisational culture. They'll recognise that you value their feedback and contributions and so facilitating a team or organisational meeting will be easier, as it's a regular occurrence, not one which creates a feeling of negative anticipation as it must be bad news because you never speak to staff members normally.

## Recognition and Reward

While much of this book has focused on how to manage difficult conversations with staff members, it can be entirely appropriate to facilitate a conversation to recognise great performance and behaviour to a staff member who has gone the extra mile to achieve outstanding results or stepped in at the last minute to help colleagues achieve their goals. Staff members are expected to deliver against their job descriptions, performance, and training and development plans but all too often we forget to say 'thank you' and 'well done' to people when they have consistently done a good job. Just because your expectations of a staff member are very high because they're so capable, doesn't mean that you shouldn't recognise and reward their effective performance.

Recognising great performance is easy as it can be done verbally, in a one-to-one meeting, a team meeting or a wider organisational meeting. Rewarding achievement can be much harder, particularly in the public sector where budgets are not usually allocated for recognition and reward systems. Rewards do not have to be financial; they might be an investment in a staff member's development, representing the organisation at an industry event, time given to leave early one day perhaps or judging the next team or organisational cookery competition. Thinking creatively can bring great rewards to your rewards system. Ask your teams how they'd like to be recognised and rewarded for great performance and you might receive some innovative ideas which people buy into very easily. While people do like a monetary bonus, they can also enjoy a more fun away to be recognised for their great work.

**Celebrating Your Successes**
When was the last time you stopped your team or organisation to say 'thank you' and 'well done'? Not half-heartedly while some people were still on the phone but stopped everyone and

### 'When was the last time you stopped your team or organisation to say 'thank you'?

took the time to show your appreciation for the work, commitment, enthusiasm and loyalty shown to you by your workforce? So often a very short-term view of work can be taken and teams lurch from week to week and month to month, delivering, budgeting, speculating, horizon-scanning and researching. But do you stop everyone and a take a moment to say "that was a great piece of work, thanks everybody"? Or do you drive people to continue their efforts constantly and fail to recognise specific successes? If a piece of work never ends how will you celebrate its success?

As an employer or line manager, the output of your organisation or team will be monitored in some form. That data supports you to recognise and celebrate the successes of your team and possibly specific staff members. What do you expect the team to achieve this month? Just more of the same of what they did last month? What will success look like then? If staff members aren't enabled to succeed because they can never exceed your expectations of them or finish a piece of work, you're unlikely to recognise or celebrate their successes and they're likely to dis-engage from you and their roles over time. That will diminish the strength and resilience of your team and potentially, the wider organisation.

As individual staff members and teams perform well, there is a tendency to increase their targets and expect more and more from them. While people can respond well to meeting targets initially, constant increases in their expected performance and delivery can have a negative impact over time. Be very wary of continuing to increase targets and expectations if successes are not recognised and celebrated, or training and development opportunities are not undertaken, as even the most driven of staff members will tire of this approach eventually. A balance between defined expectations and attainable rewards can build an effective workforce who are happy to put in the extra effort when operational challenges occur.

After reading this chapter and the rest of this book, you may well feel overwhelmed. There's a lot to do! But the intention is that you take the strategies and apply them steadily to facilitate effective changes. If you review progress in six month's time, what will have changed? There might not be huge, visible, tangible changes. Behavioural changes don't always look like that. But you, as a line manager and an effective, strong and resilient employee will feel confident and able to perform your line management role, to define expectations of performance and behaviour, tackle difficult conversations assertively and effectively, and lead a team of people who value you as their leader, just as you value them.

# Appendix A -

## Suggestions for Health and Wellbeing Initiatives

Effective health and wellbeing initiatives give staff members an opportunity to take time out, share experiences with their colleagues and to think about their own health and wellbeing. Small behavioural changes can have a significant effect on health and wellbeing over time so it's good to offer people information and allow them to pick out the aspects that are useful for them. A health and wellbeing initiative doesn't always have to be about health although a healthy baking or cookery competition can be a good option. Wellbeing can be about managing stress, feeling more confident, taking time out for yourself and giving yourself time away from your immediate work space. Ask staff members what they would like to do. In the first instance you might not get much of an enthusiastic response so go ahead and plan a few things anyway but after a while you will see more suggestions being generated as staff start to enjoy some non-work-related activities during their working day.

You must decide whether staff members will be expected to give up their time to attend specific events, such as lunch-time development sessions or quizzes for instance, or if you'll allow them time to attend. A mix of both approaches can be a good balance, to show an investment in staff members and their health and wellbeing, and a reasonable expectation that staff use their own time, such as a lunch break to attend an event in which they're interested.

Suggestions for health and wellbeing initiatives are detailed below but please note that the organisations and websites listed are given as suggestions, not as an endorsement of their content.

- **Encouraging staff members to be more active.**
Get Britain Standing (www.getbritainstanding.org) explain the impact of our increasingly sedentary lifestyles and have a range of suggestions for office-based workers to spend more time on their feet to include standing at the back of a presentation instead of sitting down and having standing or

walking meetings.

By giving people information, they can decide how they'll apply it.

- **Health and wellbeing lunchtime sessions.**
  Ask staff across the organisation if anyone has an interest in health and wellbeing topics which might include nutrition, therapies, self-development and exercise.  Arrange for presentations to be delivered in lunchtime slots and let attendees take their lunches with them if they'd like to attend.  This can be a great way for a staff member to build their confidence in the delivery of presentations, as they can start with a topic they're interested in and present to people they already know and who are likely to support their success.  Win-win.

- **Baking or cookery competition.**
  Baking and cookery challenges can take a range of forms; they don't need to just be about cake although that for -mat does seem to work very well!  Staff members might decide to add a healthy eating element or theme to the challenge and judging can be completed either by a selected panel (try not to just go with the Managers, get a range of judges across the organisation), or can be voted for by people eating the healthy delights.
  Adding a charity element to this challenge is a great way to motivate people to contribute and letting the winner decide on the charity to receive the donations can be a good way to encourage people to take part too.

- **Supporting charity events e.g.** Macmillan Coffee Morning.
  Supporting charity events can also involve baking but can be extended to office competitions, quizzes and exercise challenges.  Major charity events such as Comic Relief, the Macmillan Coffee Morning and Children in Need are a great way to bring staff members together, encourage team work between staff members who don't usually work together and build a sense of pride when money is raised and sent to the charity.  The bigger charities often provide fund-raising packs which can be a great way of starting   the conversation  as to what

© 2019 Karen Warren **195**

activities you'll undertake. Staff members might also have local charities that they like to support for specific reasons and drawing out some of those stories can bring the team together to offer support and raise money.

- **Issue a range of health and wellbeing information**
  It's important not to overload people with health and wellbeing information and emails as they lose their impact if they're seen as a nuisance but updates can be issued monthly for instance to offer information to support the health and wellbeing of staff members. Seek feedback from your team, possibly via a team meeting as to the frequency and value staff members perceive from the information.

- healthy eating and recipe ideas (www.change4life.ser vice.nhs.uk/change4life/recipes)

- healthy drinking and statistics on alcohol use (www. drinkaware. co.uk/alcohol-facts/health-effects-of-alco hol/mental-health/alcohol-and-mental-health/)

- high blood pressure and heart problems (www.bhf.org. uk/informationsupport/risk-factors)

- health issues pertaining specifically to women, such as pregnancy and menopause

- health issues pertaining specifically to men, such as testicular cancer and prostrate problems

- mental health issues (www.time-to-change.org.uk/time-talk-day-2019/resources-your-event)

- specific physical health issues such as www.diabetes.org. uk or www.asthma.org.uk If you have staff members who are managing specific conditions, ask if they'd be prepared to talk about how they manage their condition to a group of staff members. A trial run in a team meeting can be a good way to practice, before speak ing in front of a larger group.

- information relating to specific age demographics

- information relating to specific industries, particularly in terms of health and safety, and stress and anxiety

- general health and wellbeing news stories

- Having a running club, football or rounders team
  If you have staff members who're interested in specific sports or hobbies, try to build enthusiasm and team work by developing a club or team for that interest. Challenging a customer or supplier team can be a great way to build effective relationships with partner organisations and allowing a friendly spirit of competition to develop can help staff across the organisations get to know each other.

- Organising an exercise or activity challenge
  There are organisations that will run activity or exercise challenges for you but if cost is a limiting factor, there is a way of running a challenge for no cost to the organisation. It does take some time to set up and engage people but with a few willing volunteers it can be done quite easily. Our version of an organisational challenge is detailed below.

**Teams**
- Teams will be made up of six people of varying fitness levels, two from each group; lower fitness level, moderate fitness level and high fitness level.

- A lower fitness level is classed as currently doing no exercise or up to 2 miles of some form of exercise each week. A medium fitness level is defined as between two and ten miles of exercise each week, and a high fitness level is anything over 10 miles of exercise each week. *The fitness levels were defined to give a balance of fitness across the groups.*

- Each person within the team can submit three spells

*of exercise per week. This approach gave an equality of effort; the people in the high fitness group found it:*
*- very frustrating because they wanted to submit more spells of exercise than that but it engaged the people with a lower fitness level so it was important to find a balance.*
*- When the challenge was first set up, many of the people in the lower fitness groups said there was no point taking part because the people in the high fitness group would easily win but that was why the groups were split across lower, medium and high fitness levels and only allowed to submit three spells of exercise each week.*

- If people are on holiday during the challenge, they can catch up their spells of exercise in another week, with a maximum of 15 spells of exercise across the whole challenge, a five-week period.

- Teams should pick a captain who will be responsible for collating the team's exercise each week for submissions by Tuesday lunch time, to allow progress to be regularly reported.

- Teams should pick a team name.

**Exercise**
- Exercise includes anything for which a distance can be recorded (within reason!), to include walking, running, cycling, cross training and swimming. An activity conversion chart can be useful to help people calculate distances for other activities. We worked to an average of 2000 steps = 1 mile.

**Activity-Conversion-Chart.**
- One spell of exercise is exercise completed at one time during a day, for instance cycling to work in a morning, or in an afternoon. Going to the gym for an hour, for instance and using the treadmill, exercise bike and cross-trainer counts as one spell of exercise as each of these will record a distance.https://mywaytohealth.wustl.edu/wp-content/uploads/2015/09/

---

- A distance needs to recorded, not the number of steps completed, via a Fitbit for instance.

- If you're working outside of the gym, you'll need a way of recording  the distance you cover.

The following links might be useful.
- www.gmap-pedometer.com/?
- www.strava.com/
- www.mapmyrun.com/gb/
- If you're swimming, find out the length of the pool and you can work out the distance on how many lengths you swim.

## The Winners
- The winning team is the team who manage to travel the furthest using their three spells of exercise each week for all six team members over the five-week period.

The challenge wasn't perfect as we recognised that it takes a lot more effort to walk five miles than it does to cycle five miles and so a weighting system was developed with which some people didn't agree.  However, the important factors were that of the 75 people who took part we all moved more and consciously did more exercise during the five weeks of the challenge.  Staff members who didn't usually work together got to know each other and built good relationships and the challenge was a constant source of conversation across the organisation throughout the five weeks.  In a good way, not a disruptive way.  It brought us together and pitched us against each other and that brought a great energy to the organisation.

We were stumped as to what the winners would be given as prizes and thought we'd be lynched when the winning team were offered a woolly bobble with a '1st prize' sticker on it but those bobbles could be seen across the organisation for months and years after the challenge was completed.  One lady made sure to take hers when she left the organisation!  It made us smile, that was the important thing, we worked together to think more consciously about our health and wellbeing, and people responded really well to that, even though the prize was a bit rubbish.

This challenge might not translate exactly for your organisation but think about how you can bring people together across the wider organisation, help them get to know each other and give a structure for them to work effectively together. The results may surprise you!

## Appendix B - Coaching Techniques
## The TGROW Model

The TGROW model[104], a structured coaching questions tool, was first developed in the 1980s by Graham Alexander, prompted by the need to clearly describe his approach of questioning to organisations. It was popularised by John Whitmore in Coaching for Performance (1992) and is now the most popular coaching model in the world. The model provides a clear, understandable structure, with an acronym (TGROW) that catches the ethos and process of coaching. The model is an effective way of keeping conversations on track, particularly when discussions have become more challenging.

| T | Topic | What would you like to talk about? |
|---|---|---|
| G | Goal | What shall we focus on in the next 30 minutes? If this session goes well, what will have changed for you? What do you want to have happen in time available? What will you be doing differently as a result of it? |
| R | Reality | What's the real issue? Where are you in this? Who else is involved? How do you feel about it? Where are we now (e.g. actual vs target)? How important is the issue (out of 10)? |
| O | Options | What have you tried before? |
| W | Wrap Up/ Way Forward | What are you definitely going to do about it? What's your next step? When are you going to take the next step? What do you need to enable you to take the next step? |

**Figure 8 – The TGROW Coaching Model**

## Challenging Questions

Challenging questions can be used during a difficult conversation to re-focus the conversation, to help a staff member stop and really think about what's important to them. Anyone can get too focused on an end goal or tied up in the detail of a situation so by asking a more challenging question the conversation can be directed to a wider theme, which can help the staff member re-gain their perspective.

## Challenging questions can include:

- What do your colleagues think about this?

- How do you feel about success?

- What would you like your legacy to be, of this role and others?

- What's bugging you most about this?

- Who else is losing sleep over this?

- In 12 month's time what will you regret about this situation?

- Think about someone you admire and respect, what would they do in your shoes?

- How are you undermining your own progress?

- What's your self-care like at the moment?

- What advice would you give to someone in the same situation?

- What help do you need?

- What would you be doing next week if you won the lottery tonight?

## Psychological Approaches

Psychological approaches can be useful to support more difficult conversations as they can help to raise awareness of how an individual and other people function psychologically which can help to diffuse anger, stress and anxiety.

**Freud's Iceberg Model**[105] shows the differences between our conscious and unconscious minds and considers what we do and say versus how we think and feel. You might ask a staff member "how would you describe the difference between what you're saying and how you think and feel about xxxxx right now?".

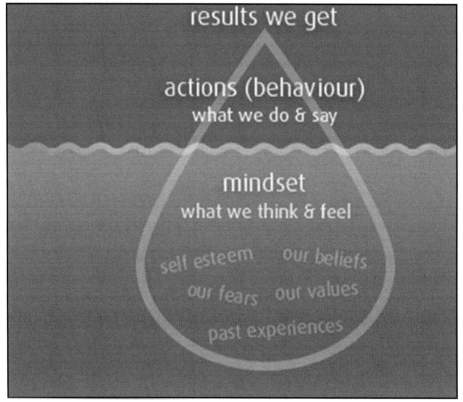

**Figure 9 – an illustration of Freud's Iceberg Model**

**Maslow's Hierarchy of Needs** defines our physiological, safety and security needs and demonstrates that without specific fundamental needs being met, an individual can struggle to build their self-esteem. You might ask a staff member, "how would you describe your current level of wellbeing? Are there any aspects of the hierarchy of needs that you're struggling with?".

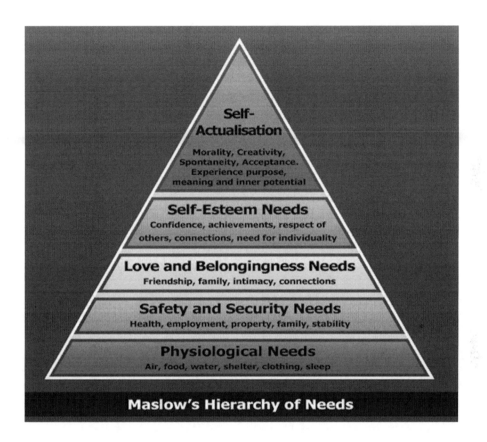

**Figure 10 – an illustration of Maslow's Hierarchy of Needs**

© 2019 Karen Warren

**Karpman's Drama Triangle** can also be useful to consider specific roles in a difficult situation and to see how drama can be perpetuated, even when one party is desperate to change their situation. You might ask a staff member "how do the roles in the drama triangle translate to this situation?".

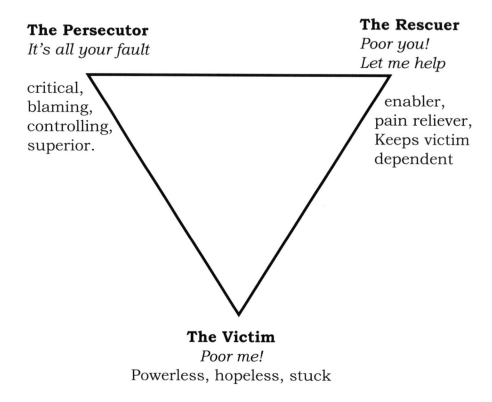

**The Persecutor**
*It's all your fault*

critical, blaming, controlling, superior.

**The Rescuer**
*Poor you!*
*Let me help*

enabler, pain reliever, Keeps victim dependent

**The Victim**
*Poor me!*
Powerless, hopeless, stuck

**Figure 11 – an illustration of Karpman's Drama Triangle**

These psychological approaches might not be relevant to every difficult conversation you encounter but having printed copies of them with you can be a great way of guiding a conversation at the right moment. Alternative illustrations of each of these approaches can be accessed online.

You can contact Karen Warren via her website kw-inner-strength.com and follow her on Twitter @KWinnerstrength

# References

1.    'Understanding the Differences: Leadership vs. Manage
      ment |Retention Planning | Tourism Info'. Go2HR,
      16 May 2017, https://www.go2hr.ca/retention-engage
      ment/understanding-the-differences-leadership-vs-
      management.

2.    The Cube, 123 Albion Street. 'An Employer's Duty of Care
      Can Manifest Itself in Many Different Ways'. Find out
      More | Acas Workplace Snippets. 4 Apr. 2012, https://
      www.acas.org.uk/index.aspx?articleid=3751.

3.    Wolfe, Lahle. 'Learn About the Importance of Having
      Written Job Descriptions for HR'. The Balance Careers,
      https://www.thebalancecareers.com/importance-of-writ
      ten-job-descriptions-3515485. Accessed 17 Aug. 2019.

4.    Bowman, Natasha. 'Do This, Not That: 10 Ways You
      Accidentally Contribute To Employee Disengagement'.
      Forbes, https://www.forbes.com/sites/forbescoaches
      council/2017/07/13/do-this-not-that-10-ways-you-acci
      dentally-contribute-to-employee-disengagement/.
      Accessed 11 Aug. 2019.

5.    *Building Organisational Resilience.* https://www.lhh.
      com/lhhpenna/en/our-knowledge/2018/Organisational
      resilience. Accessed 11 Aug. 2019.

6.    Denning, Steve. 'How Do You Change An Organization
      al Culture?'Forbes, https://www.forbes.com/sites/steve
      denning/2011/07/23/how-do-you-change-an-organiza
      tional-culture/. Accessed 11 Aug. 2019.

7.    Baker, Jodi. 'How Do You Teach a New Line manager to
      Manage?' HRZone, 29 Apr. 2010, https://www.hrzone.
      com/talent/development/how-do-you-teach-a-new-line-
      manager-to-manage.

8.    'Line manager Skills | 5 Most Important and Effective'.

© 2019 Karen Warren

Investors in People, 28 Jan. 2019, https://www.inves torsinpeople.com/knowledge/line-manager-skills/.

9. 'Employee Engagement Surveys: How Much Value Do They Really Have?' TLNT, 11 Oct. 2011, https://www. tlnt.com/employee-engagement-surveys-how-much-value-do-they-really-have/.

10. Sylvester, John. 'Top 10 Tips to Build an Engaged Work force'. HR Zone, 25 Oct. 2011, https://www.hrzone.com/ community-voice/blogs/johnsylvester/top-10-tips-to-build-an-engaged-workforce.

11. Heathfield, Susan M. 'Does Your Workplace Encourage Employee Engagement?' The Balance Careers, https:// www.thebalancecareers.com/create-work-environment-for-employee-engagement-1917575. Accessed 17 Aug. 2019.

12. Lucy, Dan & Shepherd, Catherine. 'Organisational Re silience: Developing change-readiness' Roffey Park Institute, https://www.roffeypark.com/wp-content/up loads2/Organisational-Resilience-Developing-Change-Readiness-Reduced-Size.pdf Accessed11 Aug. 2019

13. 'Following Policies and Procedures and Why It's Impor tant'. Power DMS, 2 May 2018, https://www.pow erdms.com/blog/following-policies-and-procedures-why-its-important/.

14. Delizonna, Laura. 'High-Performing Teams Need Psy chological Safety. Here's How to Create It'. Harvard Business Review, Aug. 2017. hbr.org, https://hbr. org/2017/08/high-performing-teams-need-psychological-safety-heres-how-to-create-it.

15. Denyer, D. (2017). *Organizational Resilience: A summary of academic evidence, business insights and new thinking.* BSI and Cranfield School of Management

16. 'Health, Work and Wellbeing Advice'. 5 Feb. 2008,htt

ps://www.acas.org.uk/index.aspx?articleid=1361.

17. Llopis, Glenn. 'Relationships Without Reciprocity Are No Relationships At All'. Forbes, https://www.forbes.com/sites/glennllopis/2016/02/29/relationships-without-reciprocity-is-no-relationship-at-all/. Accessed 17 Aug. 2019.

18. Psychological Safety - Management - Oxford Bibliographies - Obo. https://www.oxfordbibliographies.com/view/document/obo-9780199846740/obo-9780199846740-0154.xml. Accessed 11 Aug. 2019.

19. 'Is "Psychological Danger" Killing Your Team's Performance?' World Economic Forum, https://www.weforum.org/agenda/2016/04/team-psychological-danger-work-performance/. Accessed 17 Aug. 2019.

20. 4 Simple Ways to Make Your Employees Feel Valued. 10 June 2013, https://www.themuse.com/advice/4-simple-ways-to-make-your-employees-feel-valued.

21. Millard, Maggie. '20 Things Engaged Employees Do That Disengaged Ones Don't'. https://blog.kainexus.com/employee-engagement/20-things-engaged-employees-do-that-disengaged-ones-dont. Accessed 17 Aug. 2019.

22. 'Adverse Effects of a Bad Attitude in the Workplace'. https:// small business.chron.com/adverse-effects-bad-attitude-workplace-18249.html. Accessed 17 Aug. 2019.

23. Heathfield, Susan M. 'How You Can Best Demonstrate 1Respect in Your Workplace'. The Balance Careers, https://www.thebalancecareers.com/how-to-demonstrate-respect-in-the-workplace-1919376. Accessed 17 Aug. 2019.

24. BCI. 'What Are the Effects of Reputational Damage?' https://www.thebci.org/news/what-are-the-effects-of-reputational-damage.html. Accessed 17 Aug. 2019.

25. Reh, F. John. 'Cross-Training Employees Strengthens

Engagement and Performance'. The Balance Ca
reers, https://www.thebalancecareers.com/cross-
training-employees-2275317. Accessed 17 Aug.2019.

26. *YouTube*. 'The Good Manager' - Difficult Conversations
https://www.youtube.com/watch?v=xG2ktJ8E1mo.
Accessed 17 Aug. 2019.

27. *YouTube*. 'Employee Engagement' - Who's Sink
ing Your Boat?    https://www.youtube.com/
watch?v=y4nwoZ02AJM. Accessed 17 Aug. 2019.

28. quad rust. (2019). 'Rewarding bad behavior in workplace'.
Available: https://quadrust.com/rewarding-bad-behav
ior-in-work place/. Last accessed 17th August 2018.

29. 'Dealing With Poor Performance: Is It Lack of Ability or
Low Motivation?' http://www.mindtools.com/pages/arti
cle/newTMM_80.htm. Accessed 17 Aug. 2019.

30. 'The Effects of Poor Employees on Others'. Career Trend,
https://careertrend.com/effects-poor-employees-oth
ers-12240.html. Accessed 17 Aug. 2019.

31. 'Handling Difficult Conversations' | New Line manag
ers |LineManager Briefings | Tools |XpertHR.
Co.Uk. https://www.xperthr.co.uk/line-manager-brief
ings/handling-difficult- conversations/100052/?c=5723.
Accessed 17 Aug. 2019.

32. 'How to Become a Good Role Model' | Leadership. http://
www.thestairway.co.uk/Leadership/how-to-become-a-
good-role-model.html. Accessed 17 Aug. 2019.

33. Kohll, Alan. 'How To Build A Positive Company Cul
ture'. Forbes, https://www.forbes.com/sites/alan
kohll/2018/08/14/how-to-build-a-positive-company-
culture/. Accessed 17 Aug. 2019.

34. Cotton, P. 'How Poor Workplace Culture Can Affect Well
being'. Psychlopaedia, 26 June 2016, http://psychlopae

dia.org/?p=639.

35. '10 Ways To Improve Wellbeing In The Workplace'. Minutehack, https://minutehack.com//guides/10-ways-to-improve-wellbeing-in-the-workplace. Accessed 11 Aug. 2019.

36. Recommendations | Workplace Health: Management Practices | Guidance | NICE. https://www.nice.org.uk/guidance/ng13/chapter/recommendations. Accessed 17 Aug. 2019.

37. Display Screen Equipment (DSE) Workstation Checklist. http://www.hse.gov.uk/pubns/ck1.htm. Accessed 17 Aug. 2019.

38. PhD, Wanda Krause. 'Why a Culture of Well-Being Is Critical for Performance in the Workplace'. Medium, 8 May 2017, https://medium.com/thrive-global/why-a-culture-of-well-being-is-critical-for-performance-in-the-workplace-f6b1de08fe96.

39. Ziogas, George J. 'How To Identify Your Limiting Beliefs And Get Rid Of Them Once And For All'. Medium, 11 Oct. 2018, https://medium.com/change-your-mind/how-to-identify-your-limiting-beliefs-and-get-rid-of-them-once-and-for-all-dafa4c477a9e.

40. Swinscoe, Adrian. 'Improve Employee Engagement By Boosting Management Support'. Forbes, https://www.forbes.com/sites/adrianswinscoe/2013/11/11/improve-employee-engagement-by-helping-your-managers-get-better/. Accessed 17 Aug. 2019.

41. People Matters - InterstitialSite —People Maters. https://www.peoplematters.in/siten interstitial?return_to=%2Farticle%2Femployee-engagement%2Frole-of-communication-in-employee-engagement-14496%3Futmsource%3Dpeoplematters%26utm_medium%3Dinterstitial%26utm_campaign%3Dlearnings-of-the-day. Accessed 17 Aug. 2019.

42.    Heaver, S. 'Increase Employee Engagement by Mak
       ing Them Feel Valued'. TalentCulture, 24 Dec. 2015,
       https://talentculture.com/increase-employee-en
       gagement-by-making-them-feel-valued/.

43.    'Leadership' BusinessDictionary.Com, http://www.busi
       nessdictionary.com/definition/leadership.html. Accessed
       17 Aug. 2019.

44.    The Top Six Leadership Behaviors. https://charterfor
       compassion.org/leadership-and-business/the-top-six-
       leadership-behaviors. Accessed 17 Aug. 2019.

45.    'Kubler-Ross Five Stage Model'. Change Management
       Coach, https://www.change-management-coach.com/
       kubler-ross.html. Accessed 17 Aug. 2019.

46.    Katzenbach, Jon R., et al. 'Cultural Change That Sticks'.
       Harvard Business Review, no. July–August 2012, July
       2012. hbr.org, https://hbr.org/2012/07/cultural-
       change-that-sticks.

47.    '6 Benefits of Health and Wellbeing Programs'. Health &
       Safety Handbook, 4 Mar. 2014, https://www.healthand
       safetyhandbook.com.au/6-benefits-of-health-and-wellbe
       ing-programs/.

48.    'Challenging Conversations and How to Manage Them'
       | Acas. 16 May 2012, https://www.acas.org.uk/index.
       aspx?articleid=3799.

49.    'Understanding Workplace Values': — Finding the Best
       Cultural Fit. http://www.mindtools.com/pages/article/
       understanding-work place-values.htm. Accessed 25 Aug.
       2019.

50.    McCarthy, Dan. 'These Are the Top 10 Challenges Man
       agers Face — and How to Deal'. The Balance Careers,
       https://www.thebalancecareers.com/top-chal
       lenges-a-manager-will-face-2275955.Accessed 25 Aug.

2019.

**51.** Andersen, Erika. '9 Ways To Deal With Difficult Employ ees'.Forbes, https://www.forbes.com/sites/ erikaandersen/2013/11/21/9-ways-to-deal-with-diffi cult-employees/. Accessed 25 Aug. 2019.

**52.** Karpman, S.B. - 'The Drama Triangle and Compassion Triangle Karpman', S.B. (2014). A Game Free Life. San Francisco, CA: Drama Triangle Publications.

**53.** Miller, Jeff. 'Four Steps To Giving Effective Feedback At Work'.Forbes, https://www.forbes.com/sites/forbeshu manresources council/2018/10/25/four-steps-to-giving-effective-feedback-at-work/. Accessed 25 Aug. 2019.

**54.** Sayak. 'Benefits of Effective Listening at Work and How It Boosts Productivity'. Welcome to The HR Monks, 10 Oct. 2017, https://thehrmonks.com/benefits-effective-listen ing-work-boosts-productivity/.

**55.** McLeod, S. A. (2010). 'SRRS - stress of life events'. Re trieved from https://www.simplypsychology.org/SRRS. html

**56.** Knight, Rebecca. 'How to Handle Difficult Conversations at Work'. Harvard Business Review, Jan. 2015. hbr.org, https://hbr.org/2015/01/how-to-handle-difficult-con versations-at-work.

**57.** '6 Tips For Assertive Communication' | Impact Factory. https://www.impactfactory.com/library/assertive-com munication-6-tips-effective-use. Accessed 25 Aug. 2019.

**58.** 'UK Violence Intervention and Prevention'. The Four Ba sic Styles of Communication . Available: https://www. uky.edu/hr/sites/www.uky.edu.hr/files/wellness/imag es/Conf14_FourCommStyles.pdf. Last accessed 25th Aug 2019.

**59.** 'Empathy vs. Sympathy'. Psychology Today, https://

www.psychologytoday.com/blog/hide-and-seek/201505/
empathy-vs-sympathy. Accessed 25 Aug. 2019.

60.    Goman, Carol Kinsey. '12 Body Language Tips For
       Career Success'.  Forbes, https://www.forbes.com/sites/
       carolkinseygoman/2013/08/21/12-body-language-tips-
       for-career-success/. Accessed 25 Aug. 2019.

61.    Mcleod, Saul. 'Maslow's Hierarchy of Needs'. Simply Psy
       chology, https://www.simplypsychology.org/maslow.
       html. Accessed 11 Aug. 2019.

62.    Cialdini, R and Martin, S. (2012). *Secrets from the Science
       of Persuasion*. Available: https://www.youtube.com/
       watch?v=cFdCzN7RYbw. Video published by influenceat
       work

63.    'Scarcity'. http://changingminds.org/techniques/gen
       eral/cialdini/scarcity.htm. Accessed 11 Aug. 2019.

63B    'Factors that influence us to say yes' Cialdini and Martin
       https://www.youtube.com/watch?v=cFdCzN7RYbw

64.    'Is Heroic Leadership All Bad?' https://iveybusinessjour
       nal.com/publication/is-heroic-leadership-all-bad/. Ac
       cessed 25 Aug. 2019.

65.    'Taking Responsibility for Your Actions.' http://www.life
       coachexpert.co.uk/TakingResponsibilityYourActions.
       html. Accessed 25 Aug. 2019.

66.    Heathfield, Susan M. 'What Does Having an Open Door
       Policy at Work Mean for Employees?' The Balance Ca
       reers, https://www.thebalancecareers.com/open-door-
       policy-1918203. Accessed 25 Aug. 2019.

67.    'Problem vs. Solution Focused Thinking'. Planet of
       Success, 13 Apr. 2011, http://www.planetofsuccess.
       com/blog/2011/problem-vs-solution-focused-thinking/.

68.    'Open and Closed Questions.'http://changingminds.org/

techniques/questioning/open_closed_questions.htm. Ac
cessed 25 Aug. 2019.

69.    'Enhancing Workplace Leadership Conversations.' http://
hrmagazine.co.uk/article-details/enhancing-workplace-
leadership-conservations. Accessed 25 Aug. 2019.

70.    Lucas, Suzanne. 'Here Is How You Can Use Empathy to
Improve Your Workplace'. The Balance Careers, https://
www.thebalancecareers.com/using-empathy-to-improve-
your-workplace-4157504. Accessed 25 Aug. 2019.

71.    Building Rapport - 'Effective Communication' | SkillsY
ouNeed. https://www.skillsyouneed.com/ips/rapport.
html. Accessed 25 Aug. 2019.

72.    '10 Reasons Why Team Meetings Are Important'. Simon
Stapleton.   Com, https://www.simonstapleton.com/
wordpress/2012/04/18/10-reasons-why-team-meetings-
are-important/. Accessed 25 Aug. 2019.

73.    Power, Rhett. 'Effective Management: Extroverts vs. Intro
verts'. Inc.Com, 9 July 2014, https://www.inc.com/rhett-
power/effective-management-extroverts-vs-introverts.
html.

74.    'Sprouts'. (2018). Carl Jung's Theory on Introverts, Extra
verts  and Ambiverts. Available: https://www.youtube.
com/ watch?v=acg6HivAu5E. Last accessed 25th Aug
2019.

75.    'Employee Engagement Solutions That Empower Individ
uals.' https://www.insights.com/solutions/employee-
engagement/. Accessed 11 Aug. 2019.

76.    'How Introverts and Extroverts Can Find Harmony in the
Workplace'. Ideas, 6 June 2019, https://www.wework.
com/ideas/how-introverts-and-extroverts-can-find-har
mony-in-the-workplace.

77.    'Are You A Thinking Or Feeling Personality Type?' A Con

scious Rethink, 4 Dec. 2017, https://www.aconsciousre
think.com/6842/thinking-feeling-personality-type/.

78. Larson, Erik. 'Here's How Your Personality Type Affects Your Decision Making At Work'. Forbes, https://www. forbes.com/sites/eriklarson/2017/03/06/what-person ality-types-say-about-your-decision-making-at-work/. Accessed 28 Aug. 2019.

79. '4 Strategies You Need to Know for Working with Extro verts'. Undercover Recruiter, 1 Apr. 2015, https://theun dercoverrecruiter.com/work-with-extroverts-strategies/.

80. 'How To Manage Introverted Employees'. Officevibe, 16 Aug. 2016, https://www.officevibe.com/blog/manage-introverted-employees.

81. 'What Are Some Advantages of Diversity in Teams?' Biz fluent, https://bizfluent.com/12754775/what-are-some-advantages-of-diversity-in-teams. Accessed 28 Aug. 2019.

82. 'Managing Age Diversity in the Workplace | Reports'. CIPD, https://www.cipd.co.uk/knowledge/fundamen tals/relations/diversity/age-diversity-insights-report. Ac cessed 28 Aug. 2019.

83. 'Gender Diversity: How Men & Women Differ in the Work place'. Expedite Business Development Consulting, 9 May 2016, https://expedite-consulting.com/men-women-dif fer-workplace/.

84. 'Women in the Labour Market' - Office for National Statis tics. https://www.ons.gov.uk/employmentandlabour market/peopleinwork/employmentandemployeetypes/ar ticles/womeninthelabourmarket/2013-09-25. Accessed 28 Aug. 2019.

85. Harriss, Lindsay. 'What Is Unconscious Bias in the Work place, and How Can We Tackle It?' CIPHR, 8 Aug. 2019, https://www.ciphr.com/features/unconscious-bias-in-the-workplace/.

**86.** Pease, Barbara, and Allan Pease. *Why Men Don't Listen & Women Can't Read Maps*: How We're Different and What to Do about It. Broadway Books, 2001. Open WorldCat, http://search.ebscohost.com/login.aspx?direct=true&scope=site&db=nlebk&db=nlabk&AN=736858.

**87.** 'Tips for Managing Employees Older Than You.' https://www.businessnewsdaily.com/8676-managing-older-employees.html. Accessed 28 Aug. 2019.

**88.** Reh, F. John. 'Tips for a Younger Manager How to Manage and Motivate Older Employees'. The Balance Careers, https://www.thebalancecareers.com/how-to-manage-older-workers-2276082. Accessed 28 Aug. 2019.

**89.** Howlett, Lisette. 'Achieving Value-Add Performance Management'. HRZone, 22 Sept. 2009, https://www.hrzone.com/perform/people/achieving-value-add-performance-management.

**90.** '4 Benefits of Training and Development in the Workplace'. Big Think Edge, https://www.bigthinkedge.com/4-benefits-of-training-and-development-in-the-workplace/. Accessed 28 Aug. 2019.

**91.** Australian Government, Fair Work Ombudsman . (2013). 'BestPractice Guide Managing underperformance.' Available: https://www.fairwork.gov.au/how-we-will-help/templates-and-guides/best-practice-guides/managing-underperformance. Last accessed 28th Aug 2019.

**92.** 'Resilience in Positive Psychology: Bouncing Back & Staying Strong'. PositivePsychology.Com, 3 Mar. 2017, https://positivepsychology.com/resilience-in-positive-psychology/.

**93.** 'Stress Management Strategies.' https://www.essentiallifeskills.net/stress-management-strategies.html. Accessed 28 Aug. 2019.

**94.**   Resilience: A Positive Experience With Competent Func tioning | Cram. https://www.cram.com/essay/Resil ience-A-Positive-Experience-With-Competent-Function ing/FK5C7MAZ7MWQ. Accessed 11 Aug. 2019.

**95.**   'Five Steps to Personal Resilience.' http://www.hrma gazine.co.uk/article-details/five-steps-to-personal-resil ience. Accessed 11 Aug. 2019.

**96.**   'The Effects of Stress on Your Body'. Healthline, https://www.healthline.com/health/stress/effects-on-body. Ac cessed 11 Aug. 2019.

**97.**   Skills for Care. (2019). Building your own resilience, health and wellbeing . Available: https://www.skills forcare.org.uk/Documents/Learning-and-development/ Core-skills/Building-your-own-health-resilience-and-wellbeing.pdf. Last accessed 28th Aug 2019.

**98.**   'Are You Hard on Yourself? How to Stop Self-Critical Anxiety' | HealthyPlace. https://www.healthyplace.com/ blogs/anxiety-schmanxiety/2018/04/what-to-do-when-anxiety-makes-you-hard-on-yourself. Accessed 28 Aug. 2019.

**99.**   Warrell, Margie. 'Asking For Help Reveals Strength, Not Weakness'. Forbes, https://www.forbes.com/sites/ margiewarrell/2015/03/24/asking-for-help-is-a-sign-of-strength-not-weakness/. Accessed 28 Aug. 2019.

**100.**   'What Are the Benefits of Team Building?' https://small business.chron.com/benefits-team-building-1979.html. Accessed 28 Aug. 2019.

**101.**   'The Value of Contingency Planning.' http://www.emer aldgrouppublishing.com/learning/management_think ing/articles/contingency.htm. Accessed 28 Aug. 2019.

**102.**   'How to Change the Culture within Your Business'. Vir gin, 10 Nov. 2014, https://www.virgin.com/richard-bran son/how-change-culture-within-your-business. Accessed

28 Aug 2019.

**103.** 'How Well Is Your Workforce?' The NLP Coaching Company, https://www.thenlpcoachingcompany.com/how-well-is-your-workforce/. Accessed 29 Aug. 2019.

**104.** 'TGROW Coaching Model' Miles Downey. https://www.personal-coaching-information.com/tgrow-coaching-model.html. Accessed 11 Aug. 2019.

**105.** 'Unconscious Mind' | Simply Psychology. https://www.simplypsychology.org/unconscious-mind.html. Accessed 11 Aug. 2019.

# Further Reading

Charlesworth, Edward A., and Ronald G. Nathan. *Stress Management: A Comprehensive Guide to Wellness*. Souvenir Press, 1993.

'Helping People Take Responsibility: Encouraging Accountability'. http://www.mindtools.com/pages/article/taking-responsibility.htm. Accessed 17 Aug. 2019.

Knight, Sue. *NLP at Work: The Difference That Makes the Difference in Business,* Second Edition. 2002. Open WorldCat, https://apps.uqo.ca/LoginSigparb/LoginPourRessources.aspx?url=http://www.books24x7.com/marc.asp?bookid=4930.

Reeve, John Marshall. *Understanding Motivation and Emotion*. John Wiley, 2001.

'The Cause and Effect of Poor Leadership'. The Cause and Effect of Poor Leadership ~ Future of CIO, 22 Mar. 2015, https://futureofcio.blogspot.com/2015/03/the-cause-and-effect-of-poor-leadership.html.

# Index

dymates